The REAL WAY ROUND

1 year, 1 motorcycle, 1 man, 6 continents, 35 countries, 42,000 miles, 9 oil changes, 3 sets of tyres, and loads more ...

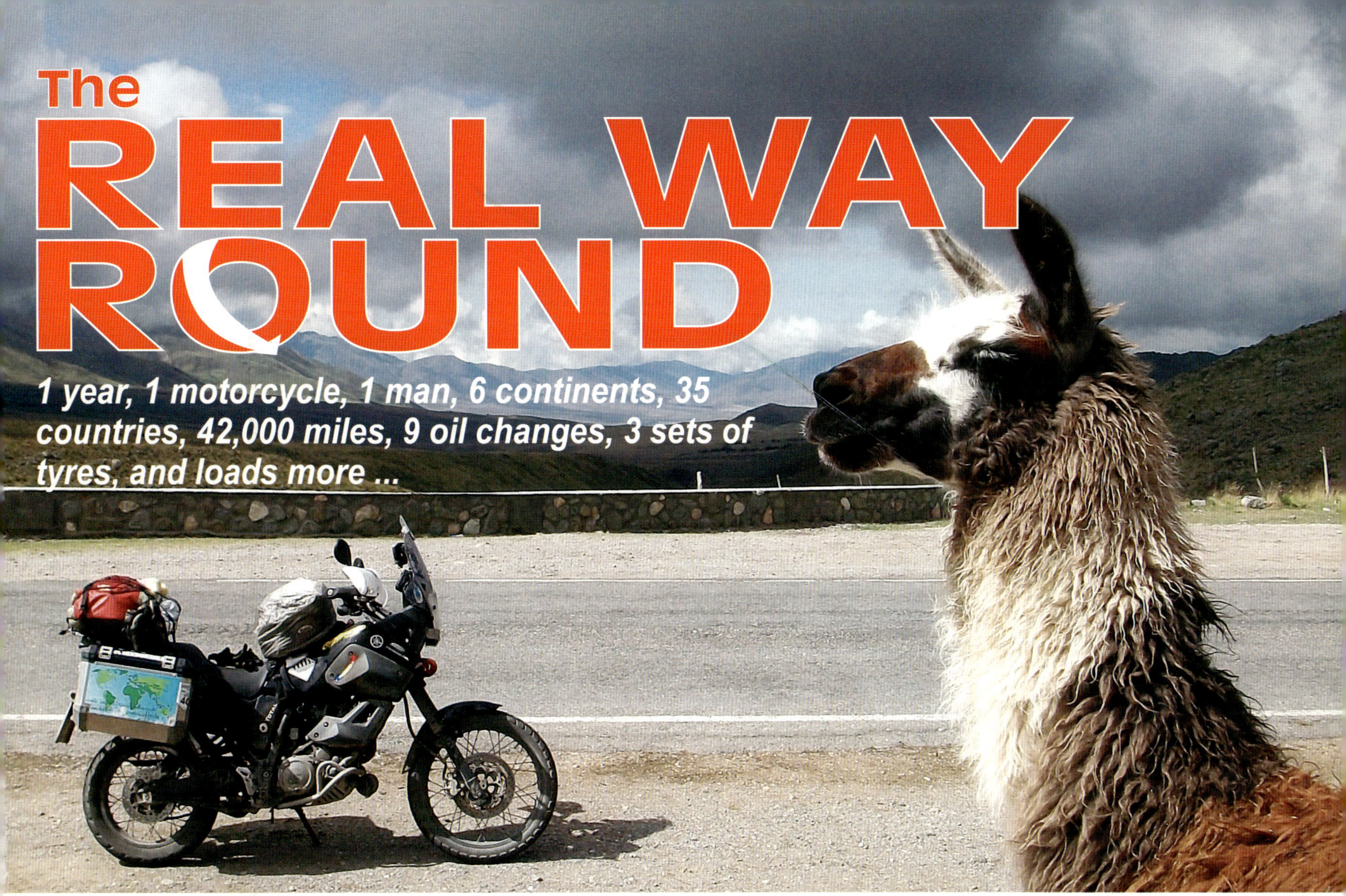

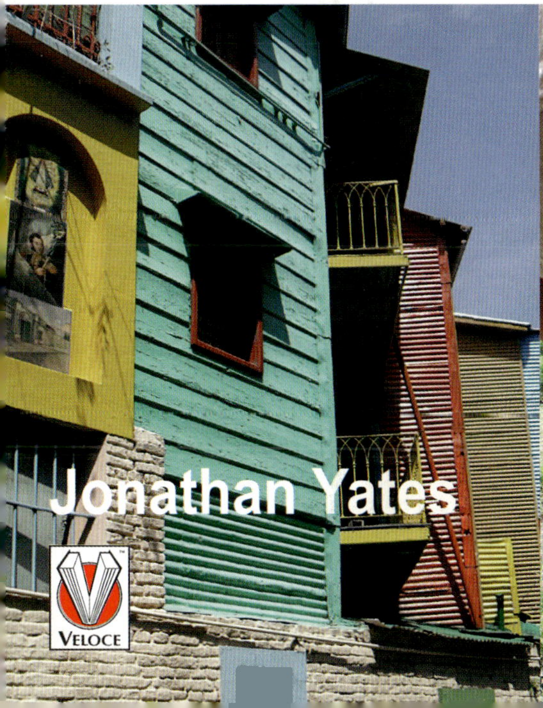

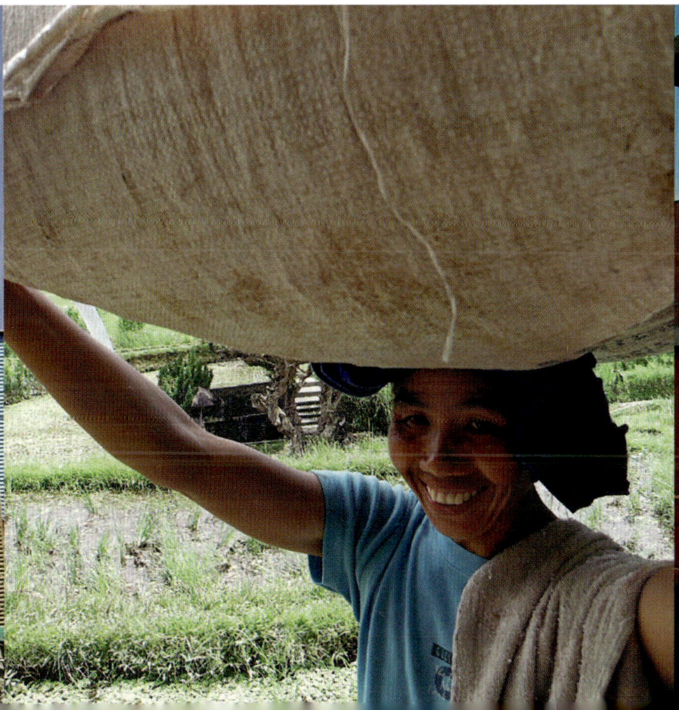

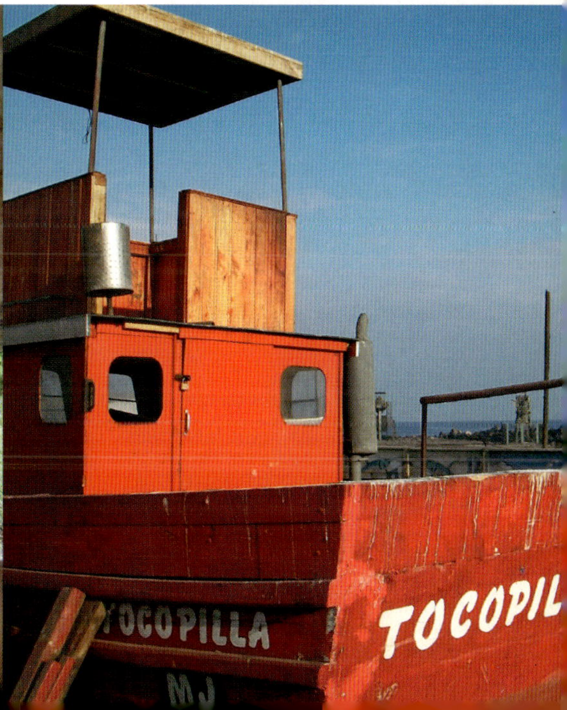

Jonathan Yates

VELOCE

RAC handbooks
Caring for your car – How to maintain & service your car (Fry)
Caring for your car's bodywork and interior (Nixon)
Caring for your bicycle – How to maintain & repair your bicycle (Henshaw)
How your motorcycle works – Your guide to the components & systems of modern motorcycles (Henshaw)
Caring for your scooter – How to maintain & service your 49cc to 125cc twist & go scooter (Fry)
Efficient Driver's Handbook, The (Moss)
Electric Cars – The Future is Now! (Linde)
First aid for your car – Your expert guide to common problems & how to fix them (Collins)
How your car works (Linde)
Motorcycles – A first-time-buyer's guide (Henshaw)
Motorhomes – A first-time-buyer's guide (Fry)
Pass the MoT test! – How to check & prepare your car for the annual MoT test (Paxton)
Selling your car – How to make your car look great and how to sell it fast (Knight)
Simple fixes for your car – How to do small jobs for yourself and save money (Collins)

Enthusiast's Restoration Manual Series
Ducati Bevel Twins 1971 to 1986 (Falloon)
Jaguar E-type (Crespin)
Yamaha FS1-E, How to Restore (Watts)

Essential Buyer's Guide Series
Alfa GT (Booker)
Alfa Romeo Spider Giulia (Booker & Talbott)
Austin Seven (Barker)
Big Healeys (Trummel)
BMW E21 3 Series (1975-1983) (Reverente, Cook)
BMW GS (Henshaw)
BSA Bantam (Henshaw)
BSA 500 & 650 Twins (Henshaw)
Citroën 2CV (Paxton)
Citroën ID & DS (Heilig)
Cobra Replicas (Ayre)
Corvette C2 Sting Ray 1963-1967 (Falconer)
Ducati Bevel Twins (Falloon)
Fiat 500 & 600 (Bobbitt)
Ford Capri (Paxton)
Harley-Davidson Big Twins (Henshaw)
Hinckley Triumph triples & fours 750, 900, 955, 1000, 1050, 1200 – 1991-2009 (Henshaw)
Honda CBR600 Hurricane (Henshaw)
Honda CBR FireBlade (Henshaw)
Honda SOHC fours 1969-1984 (Henshaw)
Jaguar E-type 3.8 & 4.2-litre (Crespin)
Jaguar E-type V12 5.3-litre (Crespin)
Jaguar XJ 1995-2003 (Crespin)
Jaguar XK8 & XKR (1996-2005) (Thorley)
Jaguar/Daimler XJ6, XJ12 & Sovereign (Crespin)
Jaguar/Daimler XJ40 (Crespin)
Jaguar Mark 1 & 2 (All models including Daimler 2.5-litre V8) 1955 to 1969 (Thorley)
Jaguar XJ-S (Crespin)
Jaguar XK 120, 140 & 150 (Thorley)
Land Rover Series I, II & IIA (Thurman)
Mazda MX-5 Miata (Mk1 1989-97 & Mk2 98-2001) (Crook)
Mercedes-Benz 280SL-560DSL Roadsters (Bass)
Mercedes-Benz 'Pagoda' 230SL, 250SL & 280SL Roadsters & Coupés (Bass)
MGA 1955-1962 (Sear, Crosier)
MGB & MGB GT (Williams)
MG Midget & A-H Sprite (Horler)
MG TD, TF & TF1500 (Jones)
Mini (Paxton)
Morris Minor & 1000 (Newell)
New Mini (Collins)
Norton Commando (Henshaw)
Peugeot 205 GTI (Blackburn)
Porsche 911 (930) Turbo series (Streather)
Porsche 911 (964) (Streather)
Porsche 911 (993) (Streather)
Porsche 911 (996) (Streather)
Porsche 911 Carrera 3.2 series 1984 to 1989 (Streather)
Porsche 911SC – Coupé, Targa, Cabriolet & RS model years 1978-1983 (Streather)
Porsche 924 – All models 1976 to 1988 (Hodgkins)
Porsche 928 (Hemmings)
Porsche 986 Boxster series (Streather)
Porsche 987 Boxster and Cayman series (Streather)
Rolls-Royce Silver Shadow & Bentley T-Series (Bobbitt)
Subaru Impreza (Hobbs)
Triumph Bonneville (Henshaw)
Triumph Herald & Vitesse (Davies, Mace)
Triumph Spitfire & GT6 (Baugues)
Triumph Stag (Mort & Fox)
Triumph TR6 (Williams)
Triumph TR7 & TR8 (Williams)
Vespa Scooters – Classic 2-stroke models 1960-2008 (Paxton)
VW Beetle (Cservenka & Copping)
VW Bus (Cservenka & Copping)
VW Golf GTI (Cservenka & Copping)

Those Were The Days ... Series
Café Racer Phenomenon, The (Walker)
Drag Bike Racing in Britain – From the mid '60s to the mid '80s (Lee)
Dune Buggy Phenomenon, The (Hale)

Biographies
Edward Turner – The Man Behind the Motorcycles (Clew)
Jim Redman – 6 Times World Motorcycle Champion: The Autobiography (Redman)

Toys & models
Britains Farm Model Balers & Combines 1967-2007, Pocket Guide to (Pullen)
Britains Farm Model & Toy Tractors 1998-2008, Pocket Guide to (Pullen)
Britains Toy Models Catalogues 1970-1979 (Pullen)
British Toy Boats 1920 onwards – A pictorial tribute (Gillham)
Diecast Toy Cars of the 1950s & 1960s (Ralston)
Ford In Miniature (Olson)
GM In Miniature (Olson)
Plastic Toy Cars of the 1950s & 1960s (Ralston)
Tinplate Toy Cars of the 1950s & 1960s (Ralston)

General
BMW Boxer Twins 1970-1995 Bible, The (Falloon)
BMW Custom Motorcycles – Choppers, Cruisers, Bobbers, Trikes & Quads (Cloesen)
Bonjour – Is this Italy? (Turner)
British 250cc Racing Motorcycles (Pereira)
BSA Bantam Bible, The (Henshaw)
Bugatti Type 40 (Price)
Ducati 750 Bible, The (Falloon)
Ducati 750 SS 'round-case' 1974, The Book of the (Falloon)
Ducati 860, 900 and Mille Bible, The (Falloon)
Ducati Monster Bible, The (Falloon)
Fine Art of the Motorcycle Engine, The (Peirce)
Ford Cleveland 335-Series V8 engine 1970 to 1982 – The Essential Source Book (Hammill)
Funky Mopeds (Skelton)
GT – The World's Best GT Cars 1953-73 (Dawson)
Italian Custom Motorcycles (Cloesen)
Kawasaki Triples Bible, The (Walker)
Lambretta Bible, The (Davies)
Laverda Twins & Triples Bible 1968-1986 (Falloon)
little book of trikes, the (Quellin)
Moto Guzzi Sport & Le Mans Bible, The (Falloon)
MV Agusta Fours, The book of the classic (Falloon)
Roads with a View – England's greatest views and how to find them by road (Corfield)
Roads With a View – Wales' greatest views and how to find them by road (Corfield)
Scooter Lifestyle (Grainger)
Singer Story: Cars, Commercial Vehicles, Bicycles & Motorcycle (Atkinson)
Triumph Motorcycles & the Meriden Factory (Hancox)
Triumph Speed Twin & Thunderbird Bible (Woolridge)
Triumph Tiger Cub Bible (Estall)
Triumph Trophy Bible (Woolridge)
Velocette Motorcycles – MSS to Thruxton – New Third Edition (Burris)
Which Oil? – Choosing the right oils & greases for your antique, vintage, veteran, classic or collector car (Michell)

From Veloce Publishing's new imprints:

Battle Cry!
Soviet General & field rank officer uniforms: 1955 to 1991 (Streather)
Red & Soviet military & paramilitary services: female uniforms 1941-1991 (Streather)

Hubble & Hattie
A dog's dinner – Practical, healthy and nutritious recipes for REAL dog food (Paton-Ayre)
Animal Grief – How animals mourn (Alderton)
Cat Speak – recognising and understanding behaviour (Rauth-Widmann)
Clever Dog! – life lessons from the world's most successful animal (O'Meara)
Complete Dog Massage Manual, The – Gentle Dog Care (Robertson)
Dieting with my dog – one busy life, two full figures ... and unconditional love (Frezon)
Dinner with Rover – Delicious, nutritious meals for you and your dog to share (Paton-Ayre)
Dog Cookies (Schops)
Dog-friendly Gardening (Bush)
Dog Games – Stimulating play to entertain your dog and you (Blenski)
Dogs on wheels – Travelling with your canine companion (Mort)
Dog Relax – Relaxed dogs, relaxed owners (Pilguj)
Dog Speak – recognising and understanding behaviour (Blenski)
Emergency first aid for dogs – Home and away (Bucksch)
Exercising your puppy: a gentle & natural approach – Gentle Dog Care (Robertson)
Fun and games for cats! (Seidl)
Know Your Dog – The guide to a beautiful relationship (Birmelin)
Life skills for puppies – Laying the foundation for a loving, lasting relationship (Mills & Zulch)
Living with an Older Dog – Gentle Dog Care (Alderton & Hall)
Miaow! Cats really are nicer than people! (Moore)
My dog has arthritis ... but lives life to the full! (Carrick)
My dog has cruciate ligament injury – but lives life to the full! (Häusler)
My dog has hip dysplasia – but lives life to the full! (Häusler)
My dog is blind – but lives life to the full! (Horsky)
My dog is deaf – but lives life to the full! (Willms)
Partners – Everyday working dogs being heros every day (Walton)
Smellorama – nose games for dogs (Theby)
Swim to recovery: Canine hydrotherapy healing (Wong)
The truth about wolves and dogs – Dispelling the myths of dog training (Shelbourne)
Waggy Tails & Wheelchairs (Epp)
Walking the dog – motorway walks for drivers and dogs (Rees)
Walking the dog in France – motorway walks for drivers and dogs (Rees)
Winston ... the dog who changed my life (Klute)
You and Your Border Terrier – The Essential Guide (Alderton)
You and Your Cockapoo – The Essential Guide (Alderton)

WWW.VELOCE.CO.UK

First published in June 2013 by Veloce Publishing Limited, Veloce House, Parkway Farm Business Park, Middle Farm Way, Poundbury, Dorchester, Dorset, DT1 3AR, England.
Fax 01305 250479/e-mail info@veloce.co.uk/web www.veloce.co.uk or www.velocebooks.com.

ISBN: 978-1-84584-294-9 UPC: 6-36847-04294-3

© Jonathan Yates and Veloce Publishing 2013. All rights reserved. With the exception of quoting brief passages for the purpose of review, no part of this publication may be recorded, reproduced or transmitted by any means, including photocopying, without the written permission of Veloce Publishing Ltd. Throughout this book logos, model names and designations, etc, have been used for the purposes of identification, illustration and decoration. Such names are the property of the trademark holder as this is not an official publication.
Readers with ideas for automotive books, or books on other transport or related hobby subjects, are invited to write to the editorial director of Veloce Publishing at the above address.
British Library Cataloguing in Publication Data – A catalogue record for this book is available from the British Library.
Typesetting, design and page make-up all by Veloce Publishing Ltd on Apple Mac. Printed in India by Replika Press.

Contents

Getting started 4	**Argentina**
Motivation for the journey 4	(including forays into Chile, Antarctica and Bolivia) . ..122
Planning: things to do and getting organised 5	
Thanks! 9	**Chile** 149
Europe	**Peru** 153
(England, France, Switzerland, Italy, Slovenia, Croatia) .. 10	**Ecuador** 160
Eastern Europe	**Colombia** 167
(Bosnia and Herzegovina, Croatia, Serbia, Hungary). .. 16	**Panama** 176
Romania 20	**Costa Rica** 179
Ukraine/Russia 25	**Nicaragua & Honduras** 182
Kazakhstan 30	**El Salvador** 189
Kyrgyzstan 39	**Guatemala** 194
China 50	**Mexico** 198
Thailand 70	**United States of America** 204
Malaysia 78	**Canada** 214
Indonesia 83	**Epilogue** 218
Timor-Leste 106	**Index** 220
Australia 110	

Getting started

Motivation for the journey

I stuffed the magazine into my backpack: I was running late and rushing to catch a bus to Hobart, Tasmania. The magazine's cover had dramatic photographs of a Thai fruit festival – men mutilating their bodies to celebrate harvest – it looked interesting so I grabbed it. It was 1997 and I was on a year out after university, backpacking round Australia.

What had seemed a pretty insignificant book/magazine swap, commonplace with all backpackers, was later to have more relevance. Within the magazine (called *Revelation*) was an article – 'Rider on a Storm' – which detailed a ride across the Nullabor (Perth to Sydney) by a solo rider who had to overcome weather fronts and rough camping, as well as face the challenge of elements of his personal circumstances, whilst riding home to meet his estranged family.

The article was so captivating that I made the same journey as part of my year in Australia: my first real road trip and a truly great journey. Previous travel in Australia had involved using public transport, or organised backpacker trips, none of which came close to the sense of freedom of having your own transport in a foreign land, providing the opportunity to really explore and get off the beaten track.

"Make progress … make progress" the instructor yelled as I failed to get up to speed on a dual carriageway during lessons in motorcycle riding in East Lancashire in 1998 (the year I passed my bike test). His squawking never really bothered me; I always rode at my own pace and have continued to do so: everyone has a sweet spot when riding, dependent on mood, conditions, and the bike.

Not much happened after I passed my test ... the AGV helmet and leather Lewis gloves gathered dust on a shelf. I did, however, continue to travel, making several short trips to Asia, including Japan, Thailand, Indonesia and Malaysia, all of which left me thinking how great it would be to escape the main tourist areas and do things in my own time. As it was, even a three week period made trips tight.

Getting started

My career took me to Leeds, and North Yorkshire provided the backdrop for the majority of the weekend rides I began to take on my bike, rolling in and out of the North Yorkshire Moors and the Lake District. I loved the simplicity of my first machine – a 600cc Yamaha Fazer which I bought in 2007.

After five years of working at J D Wetherspoon there was the opportunity to request an unpaid sabbatical. I had told a few people about my ambition to ride round the world, and they boosted my levels of anticipation by buying inspirational books related to my ramblings, such as *Jupiter's Travels* and *Mondo Enduro*. Visits to the Horizons Unlimited website (http://www.horizonsunlimited.com) and meetings were equally encouraging. Events and circumstances were colluding; the urge to do the trip increased following the Ewan McGregor/Charlie Borman *Around the world ...* documentaries. But could I do it? Was it possible to travel solo around the world? I had done only 3500 miles (5632km) on the Fazer, so was hardly experienced.

More research followed and I part-exchanged the Fazer for the new Yamaha Ténéré XT660 – a bike that boasted it could get you anywhere on a proven single cylinder engine. By this time (2008) I had made the commitment to myself – more planning was required but the decision was made: I was going to do it. I took a basic motorcycle maintenance course at Wakefield College, made some simple modifications to the bike, and applied for a one-year sabbatical from work, which was approved and began from Saturday 1 August 2009.

To be honest, the decision had been made before I even bought the Ténéré, and I had been researching possible routes for a few months, and making lists of kit necessary for serious overland bike adventure. I knew that some areas/countries were more difficult or even impossible to ride through. The Americas seemed well-travelled and accessible, but how to get from Europe to Asia, the 'Stans, China, Burma, and India?

Having one year to get around the globe did focus my plans. On my trip I met a number of riders, some of whom had similar time constraints, whilst, for others the trip had become their lives: riders four years into a road trip with no end in sight. I got the feeling some folks were just wandering: high-powered, high-plain drifters on metal steeds. I was always impressed by their stamina but did wonder what their plans were – if they had any. You meet lots of interesting travellers on the road, and they're all different people on very different journeys.

The magazine article in *Revelation* over ten years previously was the inspiration for my 'Round The World' challenge. When people asked "Why?" – and many did – the simplest and best answer was: "Why not?"

Planning: things to do and getting organised

• Budget
Keep this simple: reduce everyday costs and start saving. I think my entire trip cost £17-20,000, but it can be done for less (more rough camping/no hotels), and obviously you can spend as much as you have – there is no ceiling.

This estimate includes three air freight transportations of the bike: not sure how these elements can be reduced, and they're difficult to avoid if crossing between continents. Actual day-to-day expenditure isn't that much, especially if you're happy to camp, comparable to a year at home with bills, mortgage, insurance and weekly shopping as regular payments. What's not at all comparable is the experience!

• Solo adventure or group ride?
This is an important decision, determined by personality and how flexible your plans are. If you don't mind a few diversions because a travel companion wants to take a different route or have a day off, then riding in a small group can be fun, and allows for interesting chat about the day's ride. There are also benefits to riding solo; I think it provides a better opportunity to meet locals, who are more likely to speak to a lone person, or even offer the hospitality of a drink and meal, than if you are with a group of riders.

Luckily, I enjoyed a good mix of solo, group and couple travelling (not in a relationship!), as follows: Europe, Indonesia and the Americas – solo; Kazakhstan, Thailand, Malaysia – couple; China, Kyrgyzstan, Russia – group.

• Banking
An internet bank account is a must as you can manage your account, track spending and make transfers, etc, as you go. Get a bank card from a serious global operator, ideally with branches along the way as this can be very helpful. Have at least one MasterCard and one Visa credit card in case one or the other isn't commonly accepted in a certain country.

Try and get a bank card that doesn't charge for overseas withdrawals (persuade your bank manager to allow this) as ATMs exist in most towns and cities in all countries, which means you don't need to carry around too much cash. Ten years ago this section may have mentioned travellers' cheques, but in many ways now it's never been so easy to travel the world in so many areas, and banking is definitely one of these.

• Mugger's wallet
This is a simple wallet, containing a couple of expired cards, a few dollars and small quantity of local currency which you can produce if mugged, keeping your real money and cards in various other locations about your body or on the bike.

• Bribes
Commonplace in many countries, you should still protest a little to see if you can avoid paying, alhough, in general, it's best to just pay up and move on. Regard it as a travel tax for the epic journey you're making.

• Language
It's impossible to learn all of the different languages you'll encounter for a trip of this scale, but try and pick up as many phrases as you can from locals. Joining in with their laughter at your attempts to speak their language is a great way to break the ice.

The four Spanish lessons I had from a private tutor (found via the internet) whilst setting up in Buenos Aires were well worth it, as she was a good guide to the city.

• Communications and technology
Mobile phone: consider a sim4 travel-type card which works in a number of countries, but use only for texting as these are expensive. Buy local sim cards within countries where the time allowance – three weeks or more – merits doing so.

Notebook laptop: ensure this has Wi-Fi connectability as it allows Skype; an absolute must to keep in touch with friends and family at zero cost.

THE REAL WAY ROUND

- Keeping a log/managing photos

Set up a website that stores an unlimited number of photographs, so that if your camera SD cards are lost, damaged or stolen, all of your precious images are safe. I recommend www.dropshots.com which includes software that allows quick downloads. Friends and family can also view along the way.

- Camera

A good click-and-go digital camera with good zoom capability is adequate – anything bigger is clumsy and can take too long to retrieve and pack away. Keep it simple but take a few memory cards and a mobile hard drive which enables a second copy of photos and scanned documents to be stored. You can't be too careful: copy photos in three places – 1) Notebook 2) remote hard drive 3) www.dropshots.com.

FlipVideos are great to take short videos on and save to a Notebook or hard drive. A digital dictaphone is an excellent way of keeping an audio diary.

- Vaccinations

Begin having your jabs early as some need to be spread over a number of weeks, and don't be caught out by the rather unexpected cost of £300-plus. Malaria tablets are another £100 or so, depending on brand and how long they need to be taken for (determined by your attitude to risk and the number of affected countries you intend to ride through). Inoculations required –
- Rabies (x 3 jabs)
- Hepatitis B (x3 jabs)
- Yellow Fever (to enter China)
- Typhoid
- Diphtheria (double)
- Polio
- Tetanus
- Malaria tablets (Larium) 1 tablet per week (I did not look forward to that day)
- Other pharmaceutical items (eg repellents, Imodium, rehydration sachets, etc)

- Route planning

Get a good sat nav and practice using it. I downloaded Garmin South East Asia Mapping (£129), Argentina/Chile from the internet, and purchased cards for Australia and US en route.

Follow the news but don't be discouraged by over-reporting – 24 hour news means stories receive more coverage than they ever used to, making them seem more intense. Don't be blasé but equally don't let them put you off the adventure of a lifetime – once on the road it's simple to navigate around towns and cities where there may be trouble hotspots. If you can't avoid a town and there are no alternative routes, pass through troublespots early in the morning to minimise risk. Study maps, travel guides and online blogs (the latter is probably the most timely research you can do). Most importantly, speak to people who have recently made similar trips.

- Bike skills and knowledge

Try and get your bike a year before departure to give time to familiarise yourself with it, and to test and modify it if required.

Lots of technical colleges run basic, ten-week motorcycle maintenance courses: the one I did at Wakefield College encouraged students to bring in their own bike (working on your own machine has huge benefits) to practice changing oil/filters, removing wheels, inner tubes, electrics, etc. The course was invaluable, covering all the key areas, and gave me confidence about maintaining my bike.

Other students pointed me in the right direction to download a full manual for my bike: these can be found online for most models, and are really useful. It's also worth downloading a PDF of part numbers if you can obtain these from a bike shop or website, so that the codes of key bike parts are always at your fingertips should you need to order any.

Two key points from the course were –
- Get to know the bike you plan to travel on and complete basic but essential tasks (oil change, air filter change, puncture repair, wheel removal, brake pads) on it at least once
- Speak to as many people as you can about bike maintenance: ten minutes with the tutor before and after class discussing tools, kit, manuals, riding techniques, adjusting tools – and adding slime to the inner tubes – provided invaluable extra help and advice

The £250 cost of the course was some of the best money spent preparing for the trip. Create and laminate a simple 'cheat sheet' to use for regular maintenance and checks. There will be times when locals distract your flow when working on the bike, and having a simple list to follow helps keep the job on track in this instance.

- Bike modifications

Get to know the team at a local bike shop that has knowledgeable and friendly staff. In this respect I can't say enough good things about Colin Appleyard, Keighley, West Yorkshire. What did it help with? See following list.

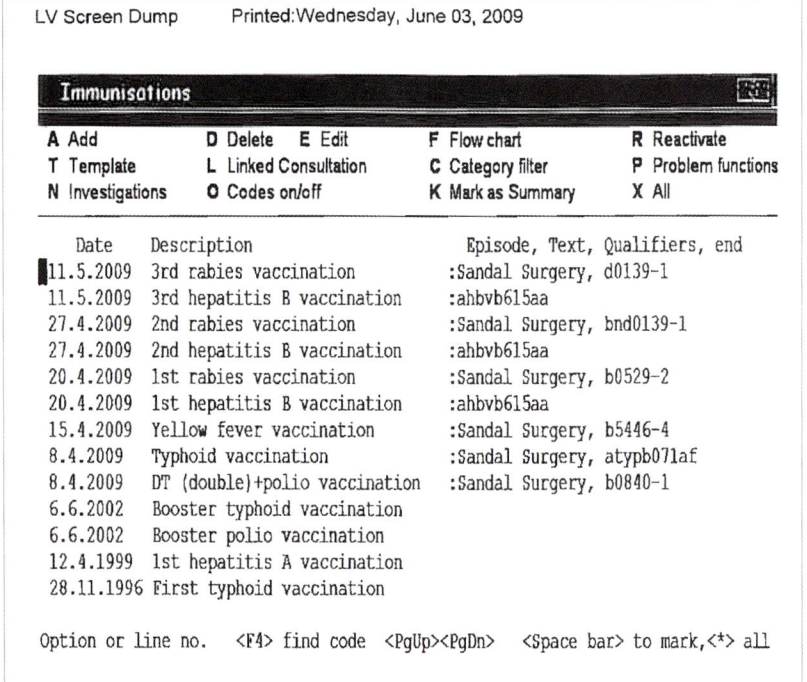

Getting started

- Tyre choice – Metzler Tourance
- Garmin Zumo 550 sat nav
- Heated grips
- Hand guards
- Bash plate
- Crash bars
- Extra-loud horn
- Large rack
- Upgrade chain and sprocket to extreme specification
- Attach spare clutch cable
- Spare bulbs
- Spare oil filters (x3)
- Spare brake pads (2 front/2 back EBC)
- Spare brake levers
- Mini pump with compressed air (x2)
- Replace existing innertubes with Pirelli super heavy duty tubes/supply spares
- Scottoiler kit
- Inner tube sealant
- Wheel nut wrench
- Spare fuses
- Puncture repair kit
- Tyre levers (large)
- Cargo net
- Sparkplugs and cases
- Chain tool
- Cable lock
- Various washers
- Motion Pro versatile tool
- Offtheroad.de pannier rack and Trax panniers
- Fairing extension
- Bike cover (use it – hide the bike)
- Rock straps
- Electrical cable ties (various sizes)
- Cigarette-style charger
- Bottle holder x2
- Headlamp lens plastic protective cover
- Tool tube and roll bag
- Spoke key
- Centre stand

● Bike kit
- TCX Infinity boots (still wear them now – outstanding quality)
- Alpinestars waterproofs (2-piece)
- Hein Gericke Toureg kit
- Goggles (never used)
- Summer gloves

● Overlanders checklist
There are lots of these available online (have a good look round). I took –
- Three season sleeping bag
- Dry Bag for back of bike
- Stuff bags
- Silk sleeping liner
- Gorilla tripod
- Leatherman wave
- iPod
- Three-quarter Gelert mattress
- Vango Banshee 200 tent
- Coleman Sporster 2 petrol stove
- Coleman mini cook kit
- Spork (fork and spoon combined)
- Casio Riseman G-Shock watch
- Large 48-page passport
- Various charging adaptors
- Blade card reader
- Various lightweight clothing
- Blister pack – those boots will rub at some point
- Spatula
- Groundsheet
- Emergency whistle
- Sink plug
- Emergency survival bag
- Mosquito net
- Water tablets
- Pocket calculator to negotiate with the border currency exchangers
- Clothes line
- First Aid kit and repellents
- Super steel epoxy
- Rhino Gaffer Tape (50 metres)

Use Tupperware boxes to store the foregoing in aluminium panniers (about 5-6 small boxes in each pannier), and carry clothes in a Dry Bag stored across the top. Pack so that you have everything necessary to hand for an overnight stay, leaving panniers and contents on the bike if safe to do so.

Always cover the bike each night; it's amazing how invisible this makes it. As soon as the cover is removed in the morning, you'll find a crowd of interested characters begin to gather to look at the bike.

● RAC Carnet de Passage En Douane (Customs document)
Issued by the RAC, this document confirms that your bike is only a temporary import and will be returning to the UK – it's essentially a vehicle passport. Most Customs officers haven't seen one before, and some countries use their own system, and don't even ask to see a Carnet de Passage. However, it is necessary in some countries, and you won't get round the world without one.

It requires a hefty deposit based on the value of the bike – I put down almost £5000 – which is refunded when the Carnet is returned to the RAC in the UK. The document is valid for a year, so arrange for it to come into force from when you anticipate reaching the first country that requires it (eg outside Europe), and not when you leave the UK.

The actual 25-page Carnet costs £150 but the main expense is the deposit. It's a good idea to order an International Driving Permit (£7) from the RAC at the same time, and I suggest you get three copies so that you

THE REAL WAY ROUND

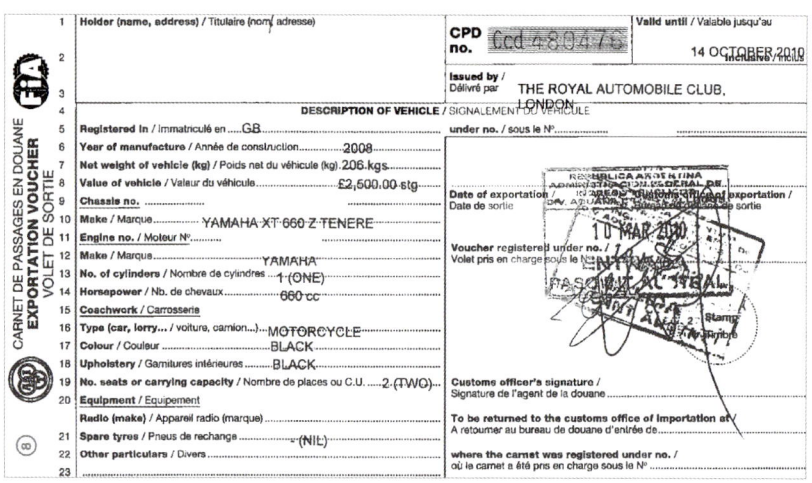

can leave spares with police, who may confiscate a document and ask for payment for its return. Contact the RAC for details.

• Insurance

Maintain your existing bike insurance as this will probably cover you in Western Europe (but check your policy). Outside of Europe some countries won't allow entry until insurance for the bike has been purchased at the border. Exactly what this covers is anyone's guess but it's needed to progress, so easier just to buy it and regard it as similar to an airport tax.

Other countries won't even check for insurance, and I would think making a claim in a country such as Indonesia is unheard of as accidental damage to a third party would be paid for in cash on the spot.

Argentina, Mexico, USA and Canada all required proof of insurance on or before entry, although only Argentina required it before the bike was released from airport authorities. I was stopped by the police in Sydney who asked to see my insurance documents: I showed them the Carnet de Passage and they gave me the okay, even though it's clearly not an insurance document.

To summarise: buy insurance where necessary, but don't over-spend on internet policies that claim to cover the bike in some developing countries. I recommend taking out a general 'backpacker' policy to insure belongings.

• Air freight/shipping

Riding overland is great fun but moving the bike by air or sea freight is quite a job. Prepare as early as possible, and make contact with the various agents before arriving at the airport. A number of tasks and paperwork have to be completed, and these vary by country, although the following are examples of some –
• Declaration of dangerous goods
• Air waybill
• Crated/uncrated/pallet
• Weight/size of bike (necessary for freight quotes)
• Disconnect the battery
• Drain fuel
• Customs procedures

• Insurance for next country (where you land)
• Shipper's declaration – dangerous goods checklist
• Confirmation of costs for release
• Temporary importation document for destination country
• Cargo release documents

• Home administration
• Sell your car if you have one, as there's no point leaving it standing for a year
• Cancel car insurance/tax
• Rent out your house/flat so that your mortgage is paid at least, and you have somewhere to come back to
• Speak to the Inland Revenue/HMRC about any rebates due
• Make a will – www.onlinewill.co.uk – (a sobering thought, but just in case)
• Gym membership needs to be cancelled early – three months' notice in most cases

• Planning whilst riding

Don't over-plan whilst in the UK. I believe there's a correlation between the length of time spent planning and the amount of money spent on unnecessary gadgets which are rarely used on the trip. Lots of planning can be done en route, and it's amazing what kit can be bought whilst on the journey.

Markets in Asia sell every conceivable tool and gadget, and if riding into colder climates there will be somewhere you can buy warm clothing if needed. Don't try and pack everything for all eventualities: yes, take some key items, but watch the budget when it comes to buying kit in the UK – gadgets look nice but don't be mesmerised by marketing from outdoor retailers.

Whilst on the road plan –
• That particular day: what key towns, how long, fuel needed
• A rough plan for the next three days
• The next month: what administration can you prep? – ie shipping, contacts, freight agents. Don't arrive at a freight company and expect it all just to happen: email contact 3-4 weeks before will enable some provisional paperwork to be organised and work scheduled

Don't over-plan on the road, either: there comes a point when it's necessary to draw a line in the sand and just go for it!

• VISA applications

These were complex and sometimes frustrating to acquire as each application form had its own idiosyncrasies. Each added to the anticipation and exciting build-up of the trip, although some were rejected initially and required amendment and resubmission.

After a number of failed applications for various countries (notably Russia and China) it seemed that a successful application may simply depend on the officer at the embassy, or the number or even standard of applications received that day – does anyone actually know? I'm not sure. The criteria for a successful visa application varied by country and seemed to change on a daily basis. However, I can say you should use the right colour ink, write in capitals, and write your date of birth in the correct order (some countries stipulate YYYY/MM/DD; others MM/DD/YYYY).

My suggestion here is to use a visa agency, which can provide invaluable advice and top tips on submitting visas, making the mountain of

Getting started

paperwork much less intimidating. Visa World (North London) was well worth a few extra pounds to check over applications, and even push them through quickly.

Alongside the agency fees, expect administration charges from the embassies, and for official Letters of Invitation for countries such as Kazakhstan.

Make sure Double Entry Visas are organised if there is any possibility these might be needed – always a good contingency should the planned route change. There are enough items that need organising before the trip without the extra stress of visa applications.

Get a new passport before you start applying (the large version with extra pages), as visa applications are a non-starter if your passport is due to expire within the next year.

It's possible – and necessary – to apply for some visas whilst on the road: I applied for a two-month visa from the Indonesian embassy in Malaysia, for example. It was lucky that I got to the embassy early, though, as my passport photo was rejected because it didn't have a red background ...

- Paperwork

Make scans of all important documents and convert to PDFs, then save to a memory stick and an email account. Make duplicate hard copies of documents and use these when possible, storing originals in Dry Bags stashed somewhere safe.

Keep making lists – and use other people's: kit lists are all over the internet, for example. When on the trip continue recording, and if you spot what you need, buy it there and then, as you might not come across it again.

Whilst riding round the world many people told me: "You are living my dream." Since returning, so many riders have said: "Wow! – that's something I've always dreamt of doing – how do you do it?"

If you are thinking the same thing, have a keen sense of adventure and good level of common sense, it's time to start planning and get riding! Motorcycling round the world is the ultimate riding adventure – the entire journey challenges riders in so many ways (both on and off the bike), but it is an achievable dream. It's simply a case of getting on with it.

Adopting a 'can do' attitude will successfully get you round the world in the greatest journey of your life!

Thanks!

Many thanks to friends and family who helped me to plan and organise my trip; all the amazing people I met along the way who made the journey so fantastic and memorable, and those who have assisted with completion of the book – cheers!

Jon Yates

Europe
(England, France, Switzerland, Italy, Slovenia, Croatia)

	England	France	Switzerland	Italy	Slovenia	Croatia
Dates in country	Fri 31 July	Sat 1-Mon 3 Aug	Mon 3 Aug pm	Tue 4-Fri 7 Aug	Sat 8 Aug	Sun 9-Tue 11 Aug
Number of days	1	3	0.5	4	1.5	3
Population (millions)	53	60	8	59	2	4.5
Capital	London	Paris	Bern	Rome	Ljubljana	Zagreb
Area (km sq)	130,000	550,000	42,000	300,000	21,000	57,000
Currency	Pound	Euro	Swiss franc	Euro	Euro	Kuna
Entry/exit points	Preston/F'lkstone (Channel Tunnel)	Calais/Chamonix-Mont-Blanc	Chamonix/Simplon Pass (Simplon)	Varzo/Pesek di Grozzana	Kozina/Podgrad	Rupa/Plitvička Jezera
Total distance miles (km)/date	500 (804)/Sat 1 Aug	950 (1528)/Tue 4 Aug	N/A	1590 (2558)/Fri 7 Aug	1685/Sat 8 Aug	1930/Tue 11 Aug
Average miles (km) per day	250 (402)	225 (362)	–	220 (354)	100 (160)	80 (128)
Maps	Sat nav	Sat nav	Sat nav	Sat nav	Tourist map (Slovenia)	Sat nav
Accommodation	Friend's house	Camping	N/A	Camping	Camping	Camping
Food	Home cooking	BBQ	N/A	Cooked meat platters	Local wine	Camp food
Value	Average	Average	Expensive	Expensive (19 euros to camp?)	Good	Good
Rating (out of 10)	5 (know it too well)	6 (much like the UK)	7 (amazing scenery)	5 (aggressive drivers)	7 (relaxed & welcoming)	8 (hard-to-beat coastline/Nat Parks)

Europe

In a nutshell
Riding Europe is easy: a bit like the UK with better weather (35°C), less traffic, miles of golden wheat fields followed by vineyards, rolling countryside and amazing mountain passes criss-crossing the Alps in and around Mont Blanc and the grand Italian lakes (Maggiore, Lugano, Como and Garda).

Things started to look decidedly different and got more interesting from Slovenia onward.

Rider notes
Bike – My experience of the first few days on the road allowed me to re-jig the packing on the bike to suit the daily routine – something that can only be perfected whilst on the trip.

Maps – (See table).

Route
France – Arnay-le-Duc, Nyon, Cluses.
Switzerland – Lake Geneva, Chamonix-Mont-Blanc (4800ft/1463m)), Simplon pass.
Italy – Lake Maggoire, Lake Como, Lake Garda, Verona, Lignano Sabbiadoro.
Slovenia – Osp, Škocjanske jame, Prent.
Croatia – Rijeka south along coast; inland to Gospić to Plitvička Jezera.

Preston-Folkestone, England
Sabbatical approved, car sold, house rented out. No going back now ...

Rider log
The departure lounge
Trip and bike preparation was undertaken in Preston (birthplace and Dad's house) because my house in Wakefield had been rented out for the past month. I left early in the morning to a single wave from the old boy; it reminded me of the first day I rode to high school, and the feeling in my stomach was pretty much the same: nervous excitement.

My passport (including the recently added Chinese visa) had to be collected on the way after finally being approved on the second or third application. I stopped at my best mate's in Greenwich for a few final beers before heading to the Eurotunnel on Saturday August 1.

I had an early start on a foggy morning for the ride to the tunnel. Eurotunnel booking arrangements are very flexible, which meant I could jump on an earlier-than-intended train – the beauty of a small vehicle. I rode off the

THE REAL WAY ROUND

tunnel in France and headed west by accident (good start), stopped; got my bearings and settled myself before continuing south-east along a number of minor roads through arable farming landscapes. The weather was great and it felt amazing. I had no destination at this stage – well, Budapest in fifteen days (which I didn't make) to meet some of the chaps I was riding across China with.

I arrived at the small village of Étréaupont with its tiny campsite that was hosting a fund raising event for the local football club (US Étréaupont). At this stage I hadn't even considered food but for 12 euros (£10) enjoyed a full BBQ, French wine, hospitality and football chat (even though this centred around Chris Waddle and Eric Cantona!) at the event. What a first day – would it always be this simple and easy?

A series of 200-250-mile (320-400km) days took me through France, Switzerland and northern Italy, arriving in Osp, Slovenia, a week later on Saturday August 8: keeping off the highways was definitely the way to go. I'd also discovered how important it was to speak to local bikers to pick up route tips and enjoy the most scenic travel by combining the two.

There is no need to over-plan for Europe as there will always be a campsite within riding distance. Begin thinking about where to camp at around 4pm each day: there's always space for one tent (a benefit of riding solo or in small groups). Rough camping was an option but I decided that there would be plenty of opportunity for that in countries with fewer facilities, so took the hot showers and other amenities when available (average cost about 12 euros/£10 a night). Roads were great; the D5 road was the best: long and twisty.

I was stumped by some very basic questions asked early on in the trip, such as "Where are you going?" My answer of "Beijing" or "Round the world" usually elicited two reactions: 1) much interest and loads of questions to the point that progress was delayed for an hour or two (it's great to meet people but you lose loads of time!); 2) their expressions let you know they thought you were either utterly mad or making it up, and they stopped talking to you.

"What's your budget?" was another such question, an answer to which, embarrassingly, I didn't have. What was my budget for the year? My plan was simple: spend what I needed to; control costs when possible but don't scrimp. The key was to find a balance and enjoy myself.

Arriving at the gulf of Venice (eastern Italy bordering Slovenia) after the first week, total mileage had crept up to 1500 (2400km). Obvious evidence of wealth at the Riviera: huge yachts and Ferraris/Porsches are commonplace – even the campsites are 'top of the range' at 20 euros/£17 a night, and packed – all of Europe is here in peak season.

Fields were full of tomatoes in Italy, and sunflowers in France. Switzerland had apricots – can't remember the area but just before Lake Geneva (I think they were apricots, anyway!). Italian drivers were the most aggressive – completely nuts. Although they may be terrible drivers, the Italians around the lakes did look good; a lot better than the French and the Swiss.

Sitting around on the bike I noticed a sign which said it was 37°C, just as a guy pulled up next to me on a Ducati, looking absolutely cool in his combat shorts, vest, and open-face helmet, an olive-skinned chick hanging on the back of him like a koala bear, wearing flip-flops and bikini, bits bobbling all over the place with the vibration of the 1098 engine – just incredible. It was a sight to compare with the scenery I witnessed crossing the Alps! I looked like I'd just walked off the Millennium Falcon from *Star Wars*, and probably smelt like Chewbacca after my nights of camping. The Italians definitely win on the style front.

Noticeable about Italy are the number of roadside signs; loads and loads of them, and every local business also has a sign. Actually trying to find a bloody campsite in the right direction or a road sign in amongst them all is nigh-on impossible. Also, pulling out of a junction is not easy because of the many blind spots that the signs cause. Still, all part of the experience …

Spotted a Yamaha dealer on the way to the Riviera and got my first bike favour of the journey when the mechanic topped up the coolant free of charge; pretty decent of him given the protracted discussion that this entailed, due to my Italian language deficiencies – you get quite a few favours when people discover what you are doing, or their store of broken English runs out.

I crossed from Italy to Slovenia on Saturday 8 August, and, after the hectic roads of Italy and over-populated beaches of Lignano Sabbiadoro,

Étréaupont, France
First camp; rather disorganised compared to later in the trip when all kit seemed to find its place on the bike

BBQ with Étréaupont FC: great guys; excellent first night

Calais-Étréaupont, France
Making hay: the first harvest. I didn't anticipate seeing so many hay bales along the way!

Osp, Slovenia
Sunflowers bordered the roads across Europe

Quaint and simple village

Simplon Pass, Switzerland
Stunning ride into Italy from Switzerland

Slovenia was an absolute breath of fresh air. A short, 90-mile (166km) ride to the sleepy village of Osp gave a total mileage that week of 1684 (2710km).

A quick trip to Škocjanske jame (a UNESCO World Heritage site) was not only a refreshing break from the daily routine of riding but – being 200 metres (650ft) underground – an ideal opportunity to escape the heat of the afternoon. The key to riding round the world is not so much about time on the bike, but having regular trips to places of interest, and days off the bike to stay fresh. Solid riding for a year will test anyone's stamina: I recommend riding for five days and then taking two off somewhere interesting.

The small campsite (only 10 to 15 people camping) in Osp was extremely friendly, and a relative of the owner gave me the details of the most scenic route into and through Croatia: follow the coast south and then head east for 200 miles (320km) to Plitvička Jezera National Park. This seemed like a good route and typical of itinerary planning whilst on the journey: keep it flexible.

West of Mont Blanc I had the choice of taking the tunnel or the Simplon Pass, and decided on the scenic route, taking the time to enjoy it. I really relished the sense of freedom this gave me, aware that in five days I was due to meet ten or so other guys in Budapest to ride with to Beijing over

the next ten weeks. This period would be very different to the approach I had taken up to now: stopping when I wanted, and going in whatever direction I fancied in my own time. Because of this I decided to delay meeting the group until Russia, giving me another week of riding solo – and complete freedom.

The difference between Slovenia and Italy is staggering. Only forty minutes inside the Slovenian border in Osp there is a feeling of complete ruralness – it's just so quiet. The campsite sold wine from its vineyard, simply decanting this into whatever bottle/vessel the customer proffered: take your own bottle and they fill it with wine – incredible. The farmland in Slovenia – and Slovenia itself – is just lovely. The roads are great for biking, and the countryside and scenery fabulous.

Travelling into Croatia revealed more of the same, but here I had my first awkward border crossing with an aggressive officer who didn't talk but shouted everything. I remained calm although felt pressured at times to produce documents and explain the reasons for my visit to Croatia. Believe it or not this was the first time I had to show my passport at a border, which the officer eventually stamped. With a final look up and down, he waved me on my way.

What a coastline, too! As soon as I'd crossed the border I stopped for a quick coffee and a couple of bananas for breakfast. The lad serving was really interested in the bike (he said it gave him goose pimples: well done, Yamaha), and was in awe of my trip. He was the third person to tell

Plitvička Jezera National Park, Croatia
Turquoise lakes set within stunning forests – looked like it could get very busy but definitely worth a visit

me I was living their dream ('don't forget how lucky you are, Jon' was the note to myself in the diary). Drinking morning coffee I programmed the sat nav, which finally found the satellite and told me that the first turn wasn't for 112 miles (180km). I had to check again: 112 miles of stunning coastline – out of this world! The road (Jadranska Magistrala or Adriatic Highway) hugged the bays, and a more nimble rider could probably dangle his right boot in the Adriatic whilst riding! I stopped and had a refreshing dip which was well worth it.

Eventually riding inland the road surface deteriorated, the linear ruts a distraction from the lightning storm visible in the distance, separating me from my destination. I put on my waterproofs for the first time. With both the storm and the bike moving pretty quickly in opposite directions, I was through in about three miles, emerging into glorious sunshine. The lightning, rain and imperfect road surface made conditions pretty hairy, although, looking back over the entire year, this was a very minor event within the context of the entire trip.

The area around Plitvička Jezera is stunning, the deep green woodlands a sharp contrast to the hot coastline, with the lakes being the main attraction. Ten days after crossing the Channel (Monday 10 August), and with a total mileage of 1939/3120km, travelling in temperatures reaching 37°C, I rewarded myself with a rest day in which to wander around the National Park. The park is a series of five or six lakes that run into each other, and the uniqueness of the area's ecological make-up, and its clear turquoise lakes and waterfalls, have made it a UNESCO World Heritage site. It is simply stunning.

Back at camp I befriended a lovely Italian couple (Luca and Francesca), travelling on a KTM. It was nice being at a campsite for two days as it provided a good opportunity to set up properly, get the stove out, buy some food, and meet some like-minded overlanders. The problem with staying just one night is the tent is down only a few hours after being put up, and there's little chance to go exploring.

In Croatia, euros are rarely accepted as legal tender, which was a surprise to me. The country has its own currency (which I didn't have any of), but I managed to get by using my cards (most shops and stations took Visa debit cards).

Thus far I'd been route planning about two days in advance, however, online searches for campsites in Bosnia kept throwing up only prisoner-of-war camps and other war-related news articles.

Eastern Europe
(Bosnia and Herzegovina, Croatia, Serbia, Hungary)

	Bosnia and Herzegovina	Serbia	Hungary
Dates in country	Tue 11 Aug	Wed 12 Aug	Wed 12 Aug
Number of days	1	0.75	2 hours
Population (millions)	4.5	10	10
Capital	Sarajevo	Belgrade	Budapest
Area (km sq)	52,000	90,000	95,000
Currency	Convertible marka	Serbia dinar	Forint
Entry/exit points	Bihac/Derventa	Odžaci/Horgoš	Horgoš/Makó
Total distance miles (km)/date	2130 (3427)/Tue 11 Aug	2300 (3701)/Wed 12 Aug	2340 (3765)/Wed 12 Aug
Average miles (km) per day	200 (321)	120 (193)	40 (64)
Maps	Limited sat nav mapping	None	Not needed
Accommodation	N/A	N/A	N/A
Food	Fruit pie (tufahije) goes well with coffee	Road snacks only	N/A
Value	Cheap although not much on offer	Cheap fuel	N/A (didn't buy anything)
Rating (out of 10)	8 (surprisingly scenic with a twist of war)	6 (straightforward and easy)	only skipped through so difficult to score

In a nutshell
This was a quick blast across Eastern Europe to Romania, overnighting in Croatia (covered in previous chapter). Bosnia and Herzegovina was one of the most interesting countries to visit; obvious signs of the aftermath of war contrasting sharply with the rugged countryside. Serbia and Hungary were straightforward rides to get to Romania.

Rider notes
Bike – No issues during these early stages, apart from getting used to putting mobile phone, iPod, etc, on charge whilst riding.
Maps – (See table).

Bihac to Orašje, Bosnia and Herzegovina
Battered rolling stock flanked the roads across northern Bosnia and Herzegovina

Get your five a day whilst on the road: eat healthily whenever possible – fruit is great value

Route

I crossed into Bosnia and Herzegovina at Bihac and headed east, slipping into Croatia, then crossing the northwest corner of Serbia (Sombor-Subotica) into Hungary. A couple of hours' riding brings you to Romania.

Rider log

It was a short ride from Plitvička Jezera to the Bosnia and Herzegovinan border, and a friendly crossing that I was simply waved through after a brief chat with the officials in their military uniforms. I hadn't planned to ride through Bosnia and Herzegovina – the original intent was to be further north – but as I wasn't meeting the others in Budapest after all, it made sense to just head east. The truckers at the border were big chaps – the eastern European man-mould is larger than that in the west – and it was easy to imagine that, before becoming truckers, these big old lads had been shot putters! (note to self: stop stereotyping, Jon).

Once across the border the farms and orchards were full of old ladies picking up fruit on the ground following the heavy storm of the previous night. In other countries (to the west) the fruit may have been left to rot but not in Bosnia and Herzegovina, which is clearly a poor country, which the road to Bihac confirmed: nothing worked in a number of towns – and certainly none of the traffic lights. Towns without power just a few hours from Italy? It seems like Bosnia and Herzegovina is almost on its knees from the ruinous war of the early to mid 90s. It may have been that the towns I rode through were particularly run down but, on reflection, I very much doubt it.

Once out of town the ride was really stunning, along the River Sava (or one of its tributaries), criss-crossing over a railway track lots of times, the road and river lovely with no other tourists in sight, making me feel like an explorer or adventurer. The same road took me all the way to Bosanska Krupa and Bosanski Novi (Novi Grad), the river on one side and the train track the other,

on which sat lots of rolling stock: unused for years and left to rust. I saw a couple of old friends, though: a Yugo and Ford Escort Mark 1 (my dad had an Escort before he upgraded to an Avenger). Bosnia and Herzegovina was like going back to the '70s in the UK!

There was absolutely no sat nav mapping for Bosnia and Herzegovina,

THE REAL WAY ROUND

so I had to rely on the tourist map I'd picked up in Croatia, which had tiny bits of north Bosnia and Herzegovina on the bottom. I used this and the river (the only reference point on the sat nav) to get myself to the next towns, and then asked for directions, with the help of a mini world atlas and lots of pointing. The first place I needed to get to was Bosanska Krupa, and asking for directions turned into a bit of a nightmare, as pretty soon there were ten blokes round the bike, arguing which was the best route to head north back into Croatia. I listened to the discussion as carefully as I could, and, despite what was rather confusing guidance, did get there in the end.

The most interesting part of the ride, though, occurred near Bosanska Gradiška, where I took a right just before the town and followed a much smaller road along the border and River Sava. For the last hundred or so miles in Bosnia and Herzegovina, all I saw were burnt-out, bombed houses, casualties of the war, and pretty scary stuff. That this was all still there was quite shocking, reaffirming the country's need of support from its European neighbours. It seemed to me that families/communities had taken it upon themselves to rebuild next to their original houses, which were smashed to pieces or had just a couple of walls standing or the frame of a roof; buildings were battered by shrapnel and bullet marks. As I rode I lost count of the small, rural villages that were completely destroyed, and the limited reconstruction that had taken place. I didn't take any pictures of the houses: although tempted to it didn't feel right, somehow. How would I feel about someone taking photographs of my burnt-out house where I may have lost loved ones?

Some houses still wore red-and-white hazard tape, indicating that live bombs and ammunition had not yet been cleared from them. One large, derelict house was covered in graffiti, yellow tape around it suggesting still-

Bihac to Orašje
Striking church and a graveyard that contains the headstones of the many young men who lost their lives during the conflict in the nineties

The majority of villages in Bosnia and Herzegovina comprised ramshackle dwellings

Eastern Europe

live ammunition, bombs or mines. It looked like it had been a key position as it was absolutely battered. There must have been some action in that house: the hairs on the back of my neck bristled.

I did take a picture of a church, noticing that all of the gravestones had dates of 1993, 1994, 1995: victims of the war; a massive loss, difficult to comprehend. As I rode I came across personal memorials built for families, and big graveyards with new headstones. It was all so weird, and really strange that so long after the war had ended, that state of disrepair still exists, without hope of a reconstruction programme anytime soon – ghost towns.

These depressing sights, combined with nowhere to stay, prompted me to make a dash north back into Croatia, and a campsite noted on my map next to Borovik Lake, en route riding through Derventa, a large town also severely damaged by the war. Near Banja Luka a number of grounded military helicopters gave an indication of just how intense the war had been.

On arrival at Borovik Lake I found a group of unfriendly fishermen intent on a drinking session, I set up a rough camp and hoped for a hassle-free evening, settling in my tent the earliest yet at just after 9pm. The day's sights had unsettled me, and I decided to keep a low profile and get an early night. Throughout the night the only disturbance were the wild dogs chasing around the tent – innocent enough, but God, did they make me jump!

The following day I whipped across the top of Serbia and ended up crossing into Hungary (unplanned and to be avoided at Horgoš/Szeged as the Serbia-Hungary border crossing was packed, and I spent more time at the border than in Hungary itself). A couple of hours later I entered Romania at Makó.

Approach to Makó, Hungary
Quick run through Hungary at dusk – good roads

Visit Veloce on the web – www.veloce.co.uk/www.velocebooks.com
Details of all books in print • Special offers • New book news • Gift vouchers • Forum

Romania

Dates in country	Wed 12-Mon 17 August
Number of days	6
Population (millions)	23
Capital	Bucharest
Area (km sq)	237,500
Currency	Leu (plural is lei)
Entry/exit	From Hungary at Nădlac; exiti into Ukraine at Siret
Total distance miles (km)/date	3795 (6107)/Fri 21 Aug
Average miles (km) per day	200 (321)
Accommodation	Camping
Food	Local sausage called a mici can be had anywhere, often cooked on grills by the roadside or in restaurants or cafés – very good
Value	Amazing, as everything so cheap. For example the cost of one campsite was around 13 lei; not more than £2.50
Rating (out of 10)	8: a real surprise with great mountain riding

In a nutshell
Dacia cars; city driving chaotic; buses run on electricity in cities like trams (lots of cables but less fumes); rolling countryside; farming; horses and carts; friendly people.

Rider notes
Bike – First oil change of trip done in Timişoara at Garage Motozone.
Maps – I bought a very good tourist map by Amco Press for 15 lei (£2.80).

Route
Timişoara: headed east to Braşov, via Voineasa Valley and Sambatta (includes route 66!). From Braşov headed north to Rădăuţi (routes 12 and 17B).

Rider log
Timişoara (third biggest city in Romania, and the starting point for the 1989 revolution which overthrew Ceausescu) was the first major city after crossing

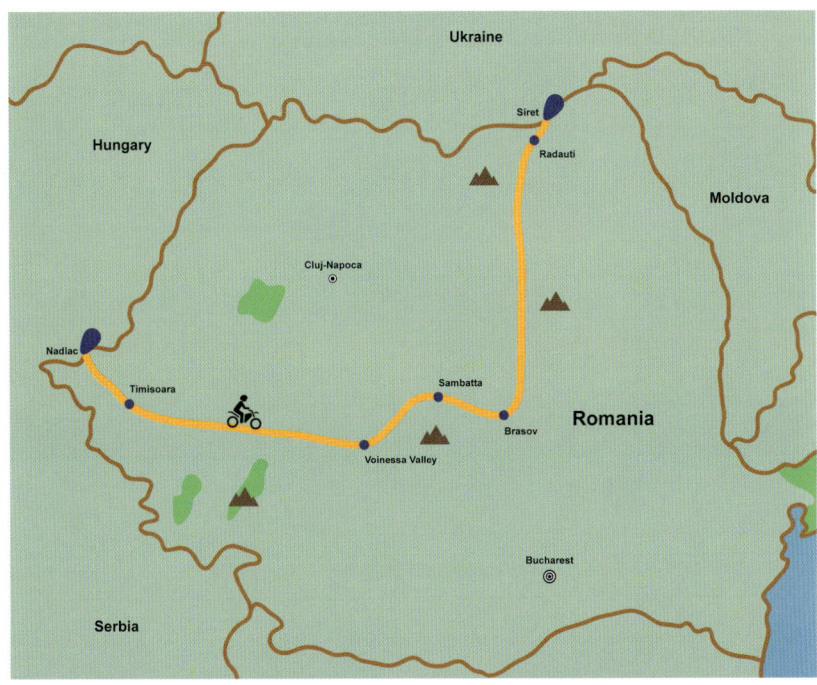

Timişoara (top right)
Paint job 1: Art on the move – a tram in the revolutionary city of Timişoara

Bicaz to Suceviţa (above)
Paint job 2: Many things seemed to be painted in Romanian colours; if something had been recently built it generally carried the EU flag. Tent and bike in top right corner

Suceviţa (right)
Paint job 3: Suceviţa Monastery: an intricately painted church

Bicaz to Suceviţa

Make hay whilst the sun shines. Lush, bright green hillsides dotted with haystacks and zigzagged with fences being used as hay-drying washing lines

Overloaded horse-drawn carts – the horses sporting brightly-coloured tassels – pick their way through the rolling countryside

Romania

the border at Nădlac. Two nights in the International Campsite just outside the city gave me the chance to plan the next few days' riding, organise an oil change, and explore the city.

Always buy a map if you see one. Luckily, I bought a map just before the sat nav failed to reboot after refuelling at the next petrol station.

After being in countries where the euro was the standard currency or I could use cards, plenty of cash machines in Romania meant I was able to get lei easily. Although in the EU, Romania is not part of the EEC. The city itself is a fabulous mix of new development and shopping centres combined with beautiful old buildings, cathedrals, and squares with café bars.

Got caught out by not adjusting my watch after moving into another time zone, which meant I was wandering around the city later than I probably should have been (only realised this in the morning). One to watch out for in the future – no hostess on this flight to tell me the local time.

In the city there's plenty of evidence of wealth and development – Romania joined the EU in 2007, and flags and bunting in many towns and cities across the country still celebrate this. Older cars carry a Romanian flag but newer ones have the EU logo. The country is really proud to be in the EU.

There was plenty of nice food, and Romania is by far the cheapest place I'd been to at this point in the trip. Breakfast at the campsite cost about £3 and comprised two eggs, four pieces of ham, a massive block of cheese, a huge tomato (and I mean huge: easily the size of a fist), and the biggest bowl of bread I'd ever seen. Outside of Timişoara the Romanian people and countryside were beautiful and enchanting. Riding through the farming valleys and across mountains was amazing: the first feeling of being totally free and somewhere different – just picking the next destination, heading towards it and finding a place to camp.

Try and aim for a 4pm finish to the day as then there is generally enough daylight to reach a decent alternative if the first place doesn't feel right (there's a lot of instinct involved here). This happened at Petrosani. I thought it would be a good place to stay on the edge of the mountain, but turns out it's a mining town with some pretty sinister-looking tower blocks for accommodation and a massive old mine. A lorry full of guys with sooty faces told me this wasn't going to be a great place to stay – just too industrial.

I asked advice from a local by making tent/sleep hand signals, and pointing to the map in the top of my tank bag. He pointed me in the direction of a place called Voineasa, and that was definitely in the mountains. The 7A road via Voineasa to Brezoi had great views but a poor surface – pot holes and loose gravel – which, at dusk, was quite difficult to pick a way through. The road then turned to dust and rubble for about 10km (6 miles), and I thought I was getting too far off track, zig-zagging up into the mountains. Then, out of nowhere, appeared a campsite with Romanian hikers. Romanians love camping and do it domestically as their cash goes further, tending not to venture into the rest of Europe. Therefore, in a Romanian campsite, you get to meet locals (locals on a global trip).

I met three great lads from the Transylvania area who referred to the revolution quite often. Guys who were only a few years younger than me were talking about a national famine, which I found extremely interesting and quite shocking in a country on the doorstep of Europe; such a contrast to the wealth I'd seen just a few days previously on the Italian Riviera. We chatted in pidgin English/hand signals and shared a beer before crashing in our tents – a great day.

Timişoara to Voineasa Valley
Forest workers concealed in the woodland would often pop out of the forest as if hijacking the bike or setting a trap; sometimes their sudden appearance from the undergrowth would startle me. The reality was they had heard the single cylinder Yamaha heading in their direction and were just curious to catch sight of the bike

I lost count of the times that I seemed to arrive at a campsite at just the right time in terms of finding a pitch – luck, planning, or just the law of averages – ride for long enough, it seems, and you will find somewhere.

Timber workers, herdsmen, horses and carts and mobile beekeepers were a feature of Romanian secondary roads. A memorable moment occurred when I met a honeybee farmer, and stopped to take a load of photos. He couldn't speak a word of English, but was really nice and showed me round his hives, truck and accommodation, really proud to show me his livelihood. I went to shake his hand and saw he had lost all his fingers: how, I don't know. I offered to buy him a drink but he wouldn't take anything, he was a really nice bloke. All the people in Romania were extremely welcoming and pleasant.

A guy wound down the window of his old, clapped-out Fiat Panda, and called to me: "Hey amigo, amigo, you go Argentina, my friend, good luck, my friend" honking his horn as he drove off. Many people wished me luck, realising from the map on the side of the bike what I was doing. A strange thing was whenever I stopped to take photos, the local kids would run get their cameras to take pictures of my bike. Odd, but so nice as well.

Voineasa Valley to Braşov
'I want my honey.' Nomadic farming – the beehives are kept in huge trailers and moved across the Transylvanian mountains

Ukraine/Russia

	Ukraine	**Russia**
Dates in country	Tue 18-Sun 23 Aug	Mon 24-Wed 26 Aug
Number of days	6	3
Population (millions)	47	145
Capital	Kiev	Moscow
Area (km sq)	604,000	17,075,000
Currency	Hryvnia	Ruble
Entry/exit points	Slobidka/Novoazovsk	Taganrog/Krasnyy Yar
Total distance miles (km)/date	4200 (6759)/Mon 24 Aug	4846 (7798)/Thur 27 Aug
Average miles (km) per day	180 (290)	170 (273)
Maps	Cartographia (Ukraine, Moldova, Belorussia)	None
Accommodation	Hotel/camping	Hotel/camping
Food	Dumplings and meat balls; seemed to like things pickled	Vodka – worth a try whilst in Russia but tasted the same as in UK
Value	Fine once camping near Odesa	Expensive: especially when you throw in the police fines ...
Rating (out of 10)	3: found the Ukraine very unfriendly/police too aggressive	4: not much friendlier than Ukraine

In a nutshell

What a shock: both countries were unwelcoming and the roads were poor.

Rider notes

Bike – Watch out for oversized potholes, dangerous vehicles, and police checkpoints which invariably mean a fine. A large number of vehicles/buses seemed unsafe – saw one car doing about 40mph (65kph) have a tyre blowout and the entire wheel came off – bouncing down the road for a mile or more.

Maps – (See table).

Ribakovka, east of Odesa, Ukraine
Iconic Eastern European statues

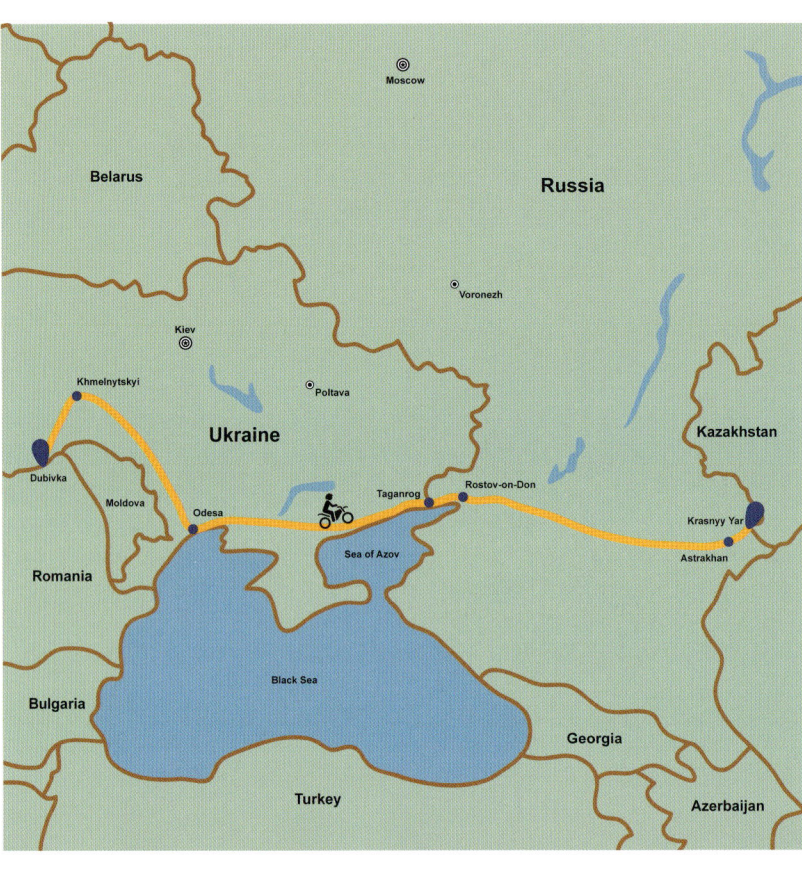

Mariupol', Ukraine
'Would you like cashback? Do you have a Club Card?' No plastic or annoying questions here; just real local shopping and organic products

Mariupol' to Rostov-on-Don, Ukraine
'I may be gone for some time.' It wasn't all beautiful scenery ...

Ukraine/Russia

Ribakovka, east of Odesa, Ukraine
Possible part-exchange for the Ténéré? It has additional baggage space – but available in 'Ukrainian blue' only

Odesa to Mariupol', Ukraine
Ukrainian vehicles are very basic

Route
Tried to minimise time on the bike due to aggressive policing, so quite a simple route. From Khmelnytskyi I headed south to Odesa, then east, following the shores of the Black Sea/Sea of Azov, into Russia and on to Astrakhan.

Rider log
At the Ukrainian border total mileage was 3117 (5016km) by Monday 17 August, following a final night camping in the garden of a Romanian B&B, run by a fantastic old French lady who made cracking homemade soup, served with a massive chunk of chicken and loads of bread. After enquiring about a shower her husband put some logs on the burner to heat the water – just magic.

I needed to push on to Ukraine as the plan was to meet my riding companions prior to entering Russia on August 24, leaving me a week to get there. Entry at the border crossing took about an hour, as the process was very thorough, and original documents only, which made me nervous (the vehicle registration documents seemed to disappear into the office for a long time). After Passport Control I was through to Customs – 'anything to declare' – and a final checkover of the bike.

I had no local currency so needed to find an ATM in the first sizable town or city. Chernivtsi, just 50km (31 miles) from the border, had ATMs in its cobbled town centre of bustling shops and cafes, though no brands or chains that I recognised. Things felt good and I withdrew 200 Ukrainian hryvnia (1 euro equals 10 hryvnia).

At the next roundabout, just outside of town, there were police in the middle of the road and I was stopped, because – they claimed – I hadn't given way or put my foot down at the junction. I knew I had done because simply seeing the police had caused me to do so. The two police officers were very young, wearing ill-fitting uniforms, and I waffled for a while, pointing to the map, pretending I was lost, in an effort to divert them. However, this didn't cut any ice and I was asked for my documents; a pointing truncheon and a big smile – gold teeth flashing in the sunshine – indicating I should get into the police car nearby.

How far could I push these guys, I wondered as I sat in the passenger seat. One handed me a piece of paper on which he'd written $100. I had dollars stashed on the bike and within the body armour of my riding kit, but I knew that if they discovered this they would take the lot. I refused the unofficial $100 'fine' and he whacked the dashboard with his truncheon a few times. This was getting serious, and enough to let me know it could get ugly. I offered him 100 hryvnia (£8). Taking my wallet he rummaged in it and took out 200 hryvnia, smiled, returned my paperwork, and sent me on my way. At the time it felt like I'd been mugged; looking back, however, I came to regard it as a tourist tax. Besides, an altercation could mean the end of my trip which I'd spent months planning.

The police were targeting vehicles with European plates – the next

THE REAL WAY ROUND

car they stopped was Italian. Expect to pay a few fines and bribes on a global bike ride.

After the paradise of Romania, Ukraine was terribly hard work. I couldn't find anywhere to camp, so rode to the outskirts of Khmelnytskyi City. In the dark I looked for a hotel, ill-prepared as I was without a detailed town map or sat nav mapping. The first hotel was full, but I eventually found another with a room on the eleventh floor: a huge disappointment compared to the campsites across Europe. It also necessitated a 'bung' to a car park 'attendant' to keep an eye on the bike – a sensible investment.

Given the police presence and their tactics, I decided to minimise the number of days on the bike in Ukraine, and located a campsite on the shores of the Black Sea just east of Odesa, spending a day and two nights at Khmelnytskyi. The 430-mile (690km) ride south east took about nine hours, and I must have passed almost 15 groups of police carrying out stop, search and fine exercises. Oncoming traffic warned of traps up ahead by flashing their lights, giving me the chance to hide behind a big truck or another vehicle before the checkpoints. As with speed cameras in the UK, vehicles would speed up once past the danger. At one trap, I glimpsed one unlucky driver with his wallet out, and remembered my experience of the previous day.

Another difficulty are the signs written in Ukrainian: some are recognisable, despite a smattering of back-to-front Rs and Ms, and a funny-looking A. It was sometimes hard to reconcile this with what was on the map whilst on the bike, so I had to stop quite a few times to study the signs against my map, at the side of some very busy roads without hard shoulders and really just a dusty, rocky track. Curbstones in towns are generally yellow and blue – very patriotic.

After speaking to other bikers we agreed that Ukrainians are not the most hospitable of people, and polite requests for directions were often simply ignored. To counteract this, the women are incredibly attractive with great shapes, so it's a case of 'directions versus distractions': take your pick! Their men generally don't seem to appreciate this, however, and seem very disgruntled. There are plenty of service stations but the attendants are rarely happy to help; one had a go at me for not filling up myself, whilst another had a go for filling up myself! I couldn't win ... None of the fuel pumps was marked, the staff either not caring or not knowing which pump dispensed unleaded fuel, so I waited for a small car to fill up to ensure I used unleaded. The card machines never work and they struggle with the chip and pin process (they have the technology but can't work it; my guess is they don't see bank cards often enough to be familiar with how to use the machines).

The last Ukrainian night was spent on the outskirts of Mariupol', rough camping on the shores of the Sea of Azov with Ron – one of the chaps with whom I was intending to ride across China, and the first time we had met. Ron directed me to the site as he had stayed there the night before, and it turned out to be an excellent find.

Following Ukraine three nights were spent in Russia with the other guys who were riding across China. The border crossing into Russia was a long, drawn-out affair, made worse by the fact that we were now a group of about ten, making us easy pickings for fines, bribes and 'official payments.' There was no consistency to this, and we were all charged different amounts: further proof of the scam.

We made the classy Rostov-on-Don after dark and the luxury of a pre-booked hotel in the companionship of other riders. One night of rough camping somewhere on the edge of Stavropol, followed by another hotel in Astrakhan took our group to the Russia-Kazakhstani border, the cultural changes and sights becoming really different and interesting at this point: Europe, as I knew it, was a distant memory.

Just across the Russian border
Simple signage: first left, second right, straight on

Rostov-on-Don to Stavropol, Russia
Get horizontal when you can and have a good stretch out
(Courtesy Steve Hotson, MotoExplorers.co.uk China Expeditions)

Ukraine/Russia

Stavropol to Astrakhan, Russia
Garmin position and summer gloves

Speed control – what better deterrent than the car of the driver who previously got it wrong, speeding round dangerous corners ...

Midway through Russia it was possible to see changes in the physical attributes and make-up of the people, and I began to recognise east Asian characteristics as opposed to those of western European peoples: very interesting.

Slight play in my bike's rear wheel caused me to stop at a Yamaha (boat/bike) dealer I'd spotted to get it looked at. The problem was the rear cush drive damper, but there was not time to do anything about it as we had to get to the border. At the dealership an eccentric customer was intrigued by our trip. After spinning his R1 round on its side stand (pretty cool), he escorted us (mostly on his rear wheel) to the border, showboating all the way, which looked good and saved lots of time. This turned out to be important as the border crossing into Kazakhstan took absolutely ages (we arrived at around 12 noon and left about 5pm. The process included –
- sign everything out of Russia
- number of check points
- passport control into Kazakhstan
- import the bike, customs declaration
- buy insurance
- a few bribes

Astrakhan to Kazakhstan border
Valentino Russia: 'Follow me, I'll get you to the Kazakhstani border'

Kazakhstan

Dates in country	*Tue 25 Aug-Sun 6 Sept (into Kyrgyzstan for 6 days) and Sat 12-Tue-15 Sept*
Number of days	*17*
Population (millions)	*15*
Capital	*Astana*
Area (km sq)	*2,700,000*
Currency	*Tenge*
Entry/exit points	*From Russia at Krasnyy Yar. Exit into Kyrgyzstan at Korday. Re-enter Kazakhstan at Karkara. Exit into China at Korgas*
Total distance miles (km)/date	*6829 (10,990) /Fri 4 Sept*
Average miles (km) per day	*125 (201)*
Accommodation	*4 nights hotel/14 camping*
Food	*Simple, but tasty soups, and beef and onion stew served with loads of freshly baked bread*
Value	*Excellent – low cost fuel (though generally low grade); excellent quality and value food; rough camping in desert free of charge*
Rating (out of 10)	*9: fabulous people, some testing riding, and fantastic rough camping*

In a nutshell

A boggy desert in places with remote villages, mixed with developed cities. The Kazakhstani people – proud, helpful and friendly – made the country one of the most memorable of the trip. September 1 is National Knowledge Day for kids, which all of the schools celebrate with flags outside – what a great idea!

Rider notes

Bike – Second oil/first filter change done in Shymkent in residential garage. A few tumbles in sand/boggy conditions.

Maps – Bought local map in bookshop which wasn't very user-friendly, as it was a very large poster without folds.

Kazakhstan

Lugovoy to Korday

Kazakhstan Soup (fuel) of the Day and hearty meals, just like Grandma used to make

Bread stall at local market (right)

THE REAL WAY ROUND

Route
Makat, Oktyabrsk, Aktobe, Irgiz, Novokazalinsk, Chilli, Kyzlorda, Shymkent, Zhambyl, Lugovoy, Korday (into Kyrgyzstan) Charyn Gorge, Koktal Zharkent.

Enter from Russia at Krasnyy Yar, exit into Kyrgyzstan at Korday, re-entering Kazakhstan at Karkara, exit into China at Korgas port.

Rider log
Despite the group splintering into smaller units to make the administration process (or lack of) bearable, entry into Kazakhstan was a long, tiring process which put us way behind schedule for the day. A group of three made it to Ganyushkino close to Atyrau (north shore of the Caspian sea). The early stages of riding through Kazakhstan were a blur of small villages with huts made of mud/sand, and many wild horses, camels and shepherds – it really was quite wild.

Three of us shared a room that cost the equivalent of $50 (£33) in a dodgy hotel, the staff clearly celebrating with the cash we gave them by partying into the early hours to American rapper Pitbull, played over and over.

Astrakhan to Makat
Remote desert dwelling

Astrakhan to Makat
Why did the camel cross the road? This was such a random sight

It was pretty annoying at the time because we'd all had a long day, but, in hindsight, it was probably the friendliest country I visited, and we should have considered the loud music an invitation to join in the dancing, maybe.

To get local currency, the next day we visited the city of Atyrau, where the contrast could not have been starker. The camels and farmers of the remote villages we had passed through were replaced by a large and developed metropolis, the one similarity being the friendliness of the people. Like the villagers, locals freely approached us to take photos; a refreshing change after Ukraine and Russia.

At the next camp we met up with Ron again, and now there were four of us ready to tackle Kazakhstan. The tricky riding conditions proved too much for our Australian compatriot, however, and he came off in a heap. After a slow recovery he and Ron split off to find the nearest city hospital (Aktobe). Turns out he'd cracked his collarbone and, with his bike, ended up getting the train to Almaty. Me and the fourth rider, Paul, continued the trip after repacking and resetting our bikes (lower tyre pressure), and we didn't see the other two again until the Chinese border.

Checking the maps we felt some pressure to get to Kyrgyzstan and then on to the Chinese border in twenty days. It was tight, as the start date of the Kyrgyzstani visa allowed about eight days to get across Kazakhstan, which is the size of Europe.

Shubarkuduk to Irgiz
Kazakhstan camps – the best of the journey. Turn off the main road, follow a track and set up camp

THE REAL WAY ROUND

Riding through Kazakhstan constituted desert/scrubland on either dirt tracks or perfect new tarmac roads, with rarely anything in-between, and it was rough camping all the way with the exception of a two-night treat in the fabulous and welcoming city of Shymkent to recover and carry out an oil and filter change, before heading off into the wilderness once more. Generally, campsites were in the middle of nowhere, punctuated by fantastic sunsets, a huge drop in temperature, and a warming sunrise. Food was simple but delicious, and a very good meal with beer could be had for less than 1500 tenge (about £5).

After Shymkent, running along the southern border the scenery and climate changed in the shadow of the Kyrgyzstani mountains to the south – this was the first time the heated grips had been flicked on, which was unexpected in Kazakhstan. Night skies were clear, and sometimes so brightly lit by stars and a full moon it was almost like day.

Across the whole of the country the Kazakhstani people were extremely friendly: for example –
- if you ask for directions they want to actually take you there
- after an oil change in Shymkent the chap asked us to dinner to meet his family
- police checking out our impromptu campsites and bikes stopped for drinks and shared our food
- drivers would pull up alongside to take photos – or go ahead of you and wave you down to stop for photos
- every village we passed the kids ran up to the bikes and wanted their photos taken, or ran alongside and waved
- at checkpoints the police shake your hand
- cars and lorry drivers toot their horns in greeting
- regular invites were received for dinner/tea/coffee
- internet café Shym City refused to take payment for large downloads
- at one garage a lad and his dad were so chatty and interested in the bikes they missed their bus – and trust me, they are not on the hour every hour in Kazakhstan
- a simple pitstop to add air to tyres ended in photos and a group hug, with ten or so excitable blokes all trying to turn on the bike and flick switches

The friendliness and helpfulness of the people was sometimes overwhelming, in fact, and all of the above instances were topped by a driver offering his CD collection as a gift.

Despite testing riding conditions in places, the bike coped very well, and a few (justified) fines didn't dampen the spirits –
- for overtaking when road markings suggested we shouldn't
- 5000 tenge fine for not getting our bikes registered (honest mistake, we thought we had done this at the border)
- 1000 tenge fine not having the headlight on (the bulb had blown)

It was good to be riding with Paul as this still gave a sense of freedom but with reassuring backup when in the wilderness of Kazakhstan. Group riding in Russia wasn't a great experience, but as a duo we were able to help each other when we came off (multiple times), and discuss routes with locals and arrive at a balanced decision.

Total mileage for the trip had reached 5596 (9005km): not bad for a month's riding.

After a month on the road this day was one of the most challenging. On the road at 7am,

Shubarkuduk to Irgiz
Land of the 'group hug'

Kazakhstan

Irgiz to Novokazalinsk
Highway 1 services. It's hard to transport a melon on a bike rack, but if it makes it to camp it's well worth the effort: four out of five melons bounce down the road and explode

Novokazalinsk to Kyzylorda
Get involved with the locals, and show equal interest in their bikes/horses/car/activity/story (whatever) as they do yours. Enjoy some banter

Astrakhan to Makat
Let's off road – hold on, THIS is the road! Highway 1: slow progress but great adventure. Don't mind admitting my relief when I rediscovered tarmac, though

between us we had come off the bikes five times; the roads were wet – sandy and bog-like – and we struggled to do 40 miles (61km). We tried to get the bikes on the back of a truck without success, so the driver laid out a rug and made a picnic for us instead! Eventually, we tiptoed our way through, hitting a decent road at around two that afternoon that we hoped would take us all the way into Almaty. I sustained my first injury of the trip when I got my foot stuck under the left pannier as the bike went over, seriously spraining my ankle and twisting my knee: nothing major but it hurt for days afterwards.

As the distance between towns grew, fuel became harder to find. There were not many petrol stations on the road, and that day we filled up with a hose from a tanker. In many stations 95 octane petrol was unavailable (all sold to the Russians, apparently) so lower grade fuel – often 92, and sometimes as low as 80 – was all that could be had.

On the final evening in Korday (near the Kyrgyzstan border) the full extent of the carnage suffered by our group became apparent –
- Adrian had broken his collar bone
- 'old' John had a suspected broken ankle
- three other guys (Mark, Joe and Ron) were missing somewhere in the north of Kazakhstan

Astrakhan to Makat

The first and only country where fuel was difficult to obtain: refuelling direct from a tanker with Ron (below)

Storing 4 litres of fuel in water bottles on the back of the bike (right)

Petrol station or petrol shed? In Kazakhstan payment is made before refuelling, generally via a little window reinforced with iron bars, after which you fill up and then collect your change (below right)

Astrakhan to Makat
Mirror, Signal, Manoeuvre: now please wash your hands. Ingenuity – everything gets reused and repaired (at least once) ...

... but look out for dodgy electrics and overflowing toilets

Only five of us made it to Korday in time – luckily we were able to meet up with those who had gone 'missing in action' on the way to China as we were entering via Kazakhstan, after six days south of the border in Kyrgyzstan. On the final night in Korday two Russian guys shared a drink with us whilst also fixing Andy's bike after he came off in Ukraine – previous repairs had failed but in Kazakhstan it was returned to full health using car spares and a Lada headlight. The people here fix and recycle everything, not like the western world where we just throw things away and generally over-consume. However I did learn from a local that her grandfather had had seven wives (it's perfectly usual to have more than one wife, apparently), and over the next few days I tried to decide whether it might be more fun to have multiple wives as opposed to the multiple gadgets found in the average UK household ...

Kyrgyzstan

Time in country	Mon 7-Sat 12 Sept
Number of days	6
Population (millions)	5: 1 million in the capital (Bishkek); majority of inhabitants are remote rural farmers, cattle breeders, shepherds, etc
Capital	Bishkek
Area (km sq)	200,000
Currency	Som
Entry/exit points	From Kazakhstan at Korday. Exit into Kazakhstan at Keng-Suu
Total distance miles (km)/date	7650 (12,311)/Fri 11 Sept
Average miles (km) per day	125 (201)
Accommodation	Home stay, yurts and hostels
Food	Kyrgyzstani mountain trout served on a hot skillet with vegetables and chips; local sweets; BBQ kebabs at roadside
Value	Seemed good
Rating (out of 10)	9: Best scenery of the trip so far, this is a rugged country, ideal for those who love outdoor pursuits. Wonderfully friendly and welcoming people. Snow!

In a nutshell

Breathtaking scenery (snowcapped mountains. amazing lakes); interesting accommodation, including homestays and yurts (a portable, bentwood-framed structure). Also some amazing riding (Silk Road historic trading routes with China). Kyrgyzstan is like the UK's Lake District on steroids!

Rider notes

Bike – Changed rear brake pads.
Maps – *State Service of Geodesy and Cartography of Kyrgyz Republic 2008.*

Route

This section was guided (arranged via the internet with MotoExplorers, a small company that brings together bikers, and assists in organising guides and paperwork for countries that have very specific entry requirements), so there was a briefing in the morning detailing that day's destination and suggested route. A support van made the same journey. A tourist travel map by Rarity Ltd was purchased in Bishkek.

Bishkek, Orto-Tokoy, south to Naryn, Tash Rabat (stone fortress), Kochkor, Dolon pass, Cholpon-Ata (north of Lake Issyk Kol), Keng-Suu.

Tash Rabat to Kochkor
Friendly farmers were often moving cattle along a road. Ride at a sensible speed, as just around the bend there may be a herd of bony cattle, goats, or stationary traffic, whose occupants have taken advantage of the roadworks to get out of their vehicle and chat!

Kochkor (bottom)
Time out at Lake Issyk Kol

Bishkek to Naryn
King of the mountains

What, no loo roll?

The border crossing into Kyrgyzstan was mad, with four lines of traffic attempting to filter through a single barrier. Keeping the bike running and ready – accompanied by lots of revving, horn-blowing and yelling – was the winning formula to muscling a way through and finding gaps. Pedestrians and lots of traffic merged with the military guards in camouflage uniform and small caps.

This was the first country that required a guide, which proved beneficial in terms of cultural knowledge, good routes and access to homestay accommodation. The next five days were spent with the guide, who was a veritable font of knowledge (apparently, 94% of the country is made up of mountains), making Kyrgyzstan an ideal destination for outdoor activities, mountain climbing, white water rafting, walking – and motorcycling, of course. The guide briefed us in the morning about the day ahead and then met us at our destination. It wouldn't be possible to tour the world in this way, but for short stints it added interest, and relieved the pressure in terms of route and accommodation planning.

Next up was a brisk, 20-mile (32km) ride to Bishkek to become acquainted with our guides and look around the city. Bishkek has thirty universities due to an extensive government education programme, and looked quite affluent, especially compared to rural areas where people live off the land.

Leaving Bishkek we headed east to Orto-Tokoy, a turquoise reservoir whose name translates to 'between forest' in English, with a backdrop of snow-capped mountains that was absolutely stunning. On the approach to remote areas the roads were unsealed.

Despite freezing temperatures, heavy rain and snow, and periods of heavy cloud cover at 3000 metres (9800ft), the views were spectacular, with yurts (portable wood-framed homes/shelters) scattered across the mountain valleys. The coldest conditions on the trip so far, I wore five layers of clothing – including thermal pants underneath my bike pants and a waterproof top – plus belt and braces, but still the wind chill factor when riding was shockingly painful as the cold penetrated the layers. The landscape and people were stunning, though, and we kept riding.

By Friday 11 September we'd covered 184 miles (296km) from Kochkor to a place called Karaköl, essentially along the northern edge of Lake Issyk Kol, which is such a size that it's known locally as a sea. Once down

cnt'd page 45

THE REAL WAY ROUND

Naryn to Tash Rabat
Whichever way you look at it, riding in the 'Stans was fantastic
(Courtesy Steve Hotson, MotoExplorers.co.uk China Expeditions)

Naryn to Tash Rabat
The most basic equipment was used to farm this huge, rugged landscape

Naryn to Tash Rabat

Weather resistant 1: Wrap up, son – gaining altitude resulted in cold riding conditions: this young chap was hardy

Weather resistant 2: 'Are your heated grips working?' Warm conversation: talk with locals; be interested

Weather resistant 3: Visor down
(Courtesy Steve Hotson, MotoExplorers.co.uk China Expeditions)

Kyrgyzstan

Bishkek to Naryn
High density living! Mobile homes – old tram carriages used as housing

Breathtaking scenery requires no caption ...

from the mountain on the shores of the lake, conditions were a complete contrast to those of the previous day, and we scrambled to lose a layer or two to stay cool. Note to self: lose layers as you lose altitude!

The latest news was that trouble in Ürümqi (local religious and cultural tensions) had resulted in communications to the area being cut off, giving rise to real concerns about getting into China. Fingers crossed all would be well when we arrived there in three or four days' time. Two English cyclists heading west reported that tension in Ürümqi was high; a potential tinderbox with a large military presence.

Leaving Kyrgyzstan on Saturday 12 September, we re-entered Kazakhstan at a place called Kapkapa. I rode to Kegen whilst the other guys went to Almaty to carry out running repairs. As I didn't need to do any work on

cnt'd page 49

Karaköl-Charyn Canyon
The 'Academy,' where a young lad learns the ropes

THE REAL WAY ROUND

Bishkek to Naryn
Yurts: mobile mountain communities. Idyllic setting and peripatetic lifestyle

Kyrgyzstan

Tash Rabat to Kochkor
Overnight snow made riding interesting the next morning – after the bike had been defrosted. Stunning scenery, complete with goat herder driving his animals across the mountainside

Tash Rabat to Kochkor
Homemade sweets being sold at the side of the road, alongside milk. After buying some we were invited into the family yurt for tea and some fresh yoghurt sweetened with sugar. To receive such hospitality was just incredible

Karaköl-Charyn Canyon
Wide loads

my bike it seemed pointless to add miles (in the opposite direction) for no reason: better to soak up the atmosphere at the next village than battle around a city, anyway. It was also nice to break from the group for a while. 'Old' John and I headed towards Charyn Gorge, fixing camp up a little track that led to a great clearing with a 360 degree mountain view, and wild horses in the distance.

Lunching at Kegen, I realised this was probably the closest I had got to the Chinese border so far in the trip, a fact reflected by the food, which we ordered by making hand gestures and animal noises for whatever meat we wanted. My stir-fry noodle soup was an obvious Chinese influence. The last few days spent pottering around the mountains and lakes had been very enjoyable; for scenic value and riding, Kyrgyzstan has got to be one of the top countries.

Some funny/scary moments were experienced, like the time I was riding behind John. The car coming towards him in the opposite direction had a farming sickle sticking out the window, which, if it had been only a metre closer, would have taken his head off!

Wednesday 16 September was a milestone day, as we left Zharkent at around 9.30am and arrived at the Chinese border a couple of hours later. In the distance two Chinese flags were visible – I had ridden to China.

True to form there is no real process when exiting Kazakhstan – it was very chaotic at the border, the officers not even beginning proceedings until four in the afternoon. Once under way, though, it was ridiculously quick and loose: lots of running about, shouting, completion of Customs forms, and official stamps for the bike and passport, plus other random paperwork that required taking to three different huts for different signatures. The actual process of exiting Kazakhstan took 30 minutes, though we had been held there for seven hours in the searing heat.

The waiting created another issue for me when, going to the loo, I was caught out. Something I'd eaten hadn't agreed with me, the result of which was I had to cut off my underpants with a knife to avoid removing my boots and pants, replacing my underwear with an old t-shirt tied like a nappy. But whilst having my 'moment' I had time to ponder the facts: I had ridden 7900 miles (12,700km) to the Chinese border with a couple of oil changes (one filter), new brake pads (rear only), only five nights in hotels and forty camping – this was indeed an adventure on a budget!

The contrast between the Kazakhstani and Chinese border points and processes couldn't have been greater. The Chinese side was like a modern airport: bags went through x-ray security checks, there was a basic health check for swine flu and a temperature check, and the bikes were held overnight for checking in the morning.

With tenge exchanged for Chinese yuan, everything was in place for the next leg.

China

Dates in country	Wed 16 Sept-Sat 17 Oct
Number of days	31
Population (millions)	1400
Capital	Beijing
Area (km sq)	9,596,960
Currency	Yuan
Entry/exit points	From Kazakhstan, Zharkent/Gulja, China. Exit via Beijing/ride to Tianjin to freight bike
Total distance miles (km)/date	11576 (18.629)/Fri 9 Oct
Average miles (km) per day	280 (450)
Accommodation	100% hotels/pre-arranged with guides and authorities
Food	Night markets and stalls for Chinese food, warm beer and a clear spirit called Jinro Soju (the latter dangerous as ABV seemed to vary). Look out for deep-fried tofu and slow-cooked soups/broths
Value	Just incredible – breakfast, dumplings hot drink and fruit 30p from street vendor. On the road food stops are incredible value, as are most things in China
Rating (out of 10)	10: hectic, contrast, dangerous roads (surface, visibility, other traffic, notably big blue buses). Unexpected cultural diversity and ethnic groups

In a nutshell

China was good – not as amazing as I had expected in terms of scenery – but the vast difference between east and west China was impressive. Each province offers something different. It was also the 60th anniversary of communism in China on 1 October, which was celebrated across the country by various events organised by the Communist Party.

Rider notes

Bike – If something needs fixing someone will be able to do it for very little cost. For example, it was necessary to grind down the side stand as the bike was too vertical when on this, due to the weight of the luggage, and had toppled over a couple of times as a result. The task was completed in seconds by a friendly chap, and at no cost. Bikes are not allowed on

Gulja
The food available night and day from the markets was sensational and great value. Crossing China on the bike meant I was able to experience a vast range of foods: and, in this respect, it really was the only way to travel

Ürümqi to Turpan City
What's for tea? In general, the food was excellent, although there were occasions when I did think: "Hmmm, this could be interesting ..."

Turpan City to Kumul
Café Real – I was always amazed by the quality of the food that came from such basic kitchens

Beijing
60th Anniversary logo

the highways, and impossible to persuade the authorities in China otherwise (bribes not taken). Maps – China-specific mapping for sat nav recommended (global mapping not sufficient for the complexities of state roads).

I used a conventional map, too: *Insight Travel Map (China, Korea & Japan)* £5.99.

Route
Entry and paperwork (Customs/traffic police) at Yining, then headed south east to Ürümqi, Hami, Wuwei, Lanzhou, Xi'an (furthest point south), north to Taiyuan, Tianjin (Tanggu), and back to Beijing.

Rider log
It was necessary to overnight just inside the

Gulja
Open All Hours: anything repaired, anytime to top standard. Nothing is thrown away – the first question is 'Can it be fixed?'

Chinese border at Korgas Post in order to complete a number of formalities. Checking the vehicle registration documents for the bikes entailed more Customs administration, but at least in China there's a sense of process compared to the flaky systems of Ukraine, Russia, and Kazakhstan. The amount of paperwork, forms, authorisations and different levels of stamps and approvals for all the documentation was staggering – so many different authorities. Even a carbon copy rubbing of the bike's chassis number was taken!

On the way to Customs the next morning people in a massive queue trying to get out of China into Kazakhstan were climbing all over each other once the gates were opened: the biggest border scramble I'd seen to date

China

Zharkent to Gulja
Body: sight test, health check
Bike: Chinese provisional licence; carbon copy of the frame number

it was absolutely mad. Everyone appeared desperate to get somewhere (back to Kazakhstan – a product of the reported regional tensions in the Western Provinces?): it may be that there was a daily quota, but these people just wanted to get out and do it quickly.

I had a couple of appointments to keep that day, Friday 18 September –
• 8.30am: police for a bike check – almost an MoT. Hard to understand when some of the vehicles I'd seen on the road looked like three or four vehicles combined. There were bikes everywhere and it was a slow process, so slow, in fact, that we got out the stove to make tea. This drew a small crowd which was quickly scattered by a man who, despite his civilian clothing, was definitely a figure of authority. Very controlled.
• 12.30pm: driving licence department and another police department for bike check and to have our photographs taken (and even an eye test before we could get our licences). We queued in alphabetical order: very organised compared to all previous countries.

The diversity and scale of China is overwhelming. Huge toll booth gates give entry to the super-highways, but the roads are unused, whilst there's carnage on the state roads in and

THE REAL WAY ROUND

Xiahe to Tianshui
Sign issues

Zharkent to Gulja
Trikes, bikes and automobiles: overloaded, electrically-powered, protected with carpets, people carriers and very wide loads. Some serious overtaking manoeuvres are required on Chinese roads

China

Yining to Kuytun
Ambitious developments were commonplace

Following the Mongolian border south east was a pretty boring ride, continually overtaking overladen trucks; hundreds in one day alone. A lot of the trucks drive on the wrong side of the road anyway, and bikes are pushed onto the gravel tracks, making overtaking especially hadardous. An average day's ride across China contains so much it's hard to know where to start. Usually departing at 8am we would arrive at our destination around seven in the evening, giving a couple of hours in which to wind down. During the 290 mile (466km) leg from Yinning to Kuytun, on September 19 we travelled on unsurfaced roads through scenic mountain passes, via a number of small villages, all of which specialised in selling or producing certain items, depending on local skills and/or resources: honey in the mountains; sheet metal on the outskirts of town; cotton clothing and fabric. One common factor, though, was that all had good local food shops and cafés.

A high level of development was noticeable most days, the scale of investment in infrastructure much greater than in any other country, none of which even came close to China in this respect. Most days we witnessed the ongoing construction of amazing bridges, high-rise flats, and other structures everywhere; the super-highways linking the cities are perfect. People, tiny dots on a vast horizon, work in teams alongside new roads all the time which have not even a crease in them. The Chinese seem to do things on a huge scale. The new highway roads are long and wide, and it was common to see another road being developed and running parallel, creating dual carriageways across this vast land. Occasionally, groups of people could be seen sweeping the roads, and I've even witnessed large numbers of labourers sweeping the main highway – surely a futile task in a sandy desert? China is a country of huge contrast: basic human/animal labouring in some parts and advanced technology in others.

out of cities as five or six vehicles try to turn right at the same time; green and red traffic lights go ignored, and vehicles drive on the wrong side of the road. The rules are simple – size equals right of way. Riding in the cities is out of control, very aggressive and chaotic – not for the faint-hearted – and can only be compared to a computer game, except second lives are not usual.

On the highways it was also hectic: not many cars but massive freight wagons to overtake. I saw at least three wagons that had gone off the edge of the road and overturned (where they are left; a sombre reminder to take care ...).

Visited early on during the trip across China, one of the more interesting cities was Ürümqi with a population of four million, at the time experiencing ethnic tension which led to problems getting our visas. Walking round the city, a strong Muslim presence is evident in faces, dress, markets, food, and buildings with Arabic writing. Not sure why tensions exist or have come to a head, but at checkpoints into the city, cars were being thoroughly searched and bags checked, with some items removed and confiscated Within Ürümqi soldiers with guns stood on blocks at each street corner, scanning the crowds, and there were also regular patrols of 8 or 10 armed soldiers, plus riot police, so all-in-all a very strong military presence. Despite this, life seemed to bumble along: one of the markets was especially nice with the usual bustle and lovely food, although not so nice was the slaughter and skinning of lambs that went on as ten or more others watched and awaited the same fate. The slaughterman inserted a hose underneath the skin of each lamb's leg, pumping air under the skin's surface to loosen it and make skinning easier. An unusual skill and rather gruesome.

Kuytun to Ürümqi (Xinjiang Uyghur Autonomous Region)
Street Life: Ritual slaughter by Uyghur shepherd. Ürümqi riots in July 2009 left almost 200 people killed and 2000 injured. A strong police/military presence existed throughout the city, and by November, nine people had been executed and a further 400 faced criminal charges for involvement in the riots. After seeing the military stop a bus and remove a group of youngsters, I wondered about their future, and how this persecution might affect their traditional way of life

The following morning just before leaving Ürümqi, the authorities were in full swing. They stopped a bus, closed all the windows from the outside so that no one could throw anything off or climb out, then boarded the bus and swept through it, removing four young people – three lads and one girl. Twenty or so policemen in riot gear and platoons of around 15 soldiers patrolled a highly monitored area of the city, giving the feeling that things could kick off at any time. It wasn't until a number of days after leaving the city that the tension – and the military presence – in Gansu province declined, and mobile and internet communication was possible once again.

Zharkent to Gulja
Markets sold fresh veg locally produced: isn't there a message here for supermarkets in the UK? Spices and eggs were plentiful

Everywhere in China it is usual for men to splt, and no one bats an eyelid. I attribute this to smoking, which is the norm. I even saw a promotion in one city where cigarettes were given away free by tobacco companies: no smoking bans here. Getting cigarettes isn't a problem but if coffee is your drug of choice, bring your own, because this is the land of tea.

Places worth seeing
China is a very interesting country, with lots to see. Some of the more touristy destinations worth a visit are –

Tianjin to Tanggu
'Pit stop teams' hand-washed the bike – and even gave it a blow dry!

THE REAL WAY ROUND

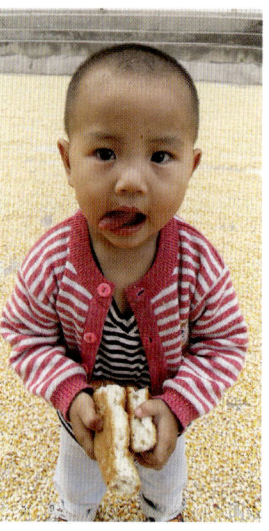

Gulja
Bread baking

Jiayuguan to Zhangye
The Great Wall

- Jiaohe city ruins: over 380,000 square metres of ancient, earthen buildings
- Turpan city (very dry: only an inch of rain a year) is based on a irrigation system built 2000 years ago. An attraction in itself, and known as the Karez, this underground water system is similar to what you'd see in Middle Eastern countries
- The ancient Suleiman Minaret mosque was fabulous. The ancient city was a heritage site dating back to 1BC, raided by the Mongols in the 13th century and then rebuilt
- Mogao Caves (a UNESCO site) are a bit pricey at £18 a visit but quite interesting. 750 religious caves, dating back to the 14th century, occupy the side of a mountain. It took ten centuries to build and finish them
- The Great Wall at Jiayuguan is the start of the Great Wall of China (just over 5000km/3000 miles), and the Silk Road (also known as 'the magnificent path'), where all the traders used to come through many centuries ago, cuts through Shiguan Gorge. The wall's main objective was to keep out attacking Mongols
- Labrang Monastery, Xiahe, is a lovely temple set in stunning scenery, the monks in their deep red wine-coloured robes making a striking picture. Some of them were really young lads, who played basketball whilst the older monks prayed, all of them under the scrutiny of a group of soldiers watching from the outskirts of the area. Two military trucks were a reminder that police and the military are never far away, and a water cannon truck complete with video photographed visitors in and out of the area. Everything is logged
- The Terracotta Army, just outside Xi'an, was bigger than expected, and draws loads of tourists (5 million per year, mostly Chinese, but a few Europeans also). There are plenty of terracotta soldiers, emperors, and horses, some of it still not excavated as the whole site only came to light in 1974 as the result of a farmer digging in the earth – an amazing discovery.
- Shaolin Temple, Dengfeng, home of Chinese martial arts and 500 Buddhas, and a massive Kung Fu school, with hundreds of kids in training

Key events: highway to state roads

Eventually we were banned from the highways as no bikes are allowed on them (the Chinese stipulate only car owners who can afford the tariffs can use these). I'm not sure how we got away with it during the first few days, and can only assume it was because of a more relaxed attitude in the first province, or

Lanzhou to Xiahe
Tianshui Temple

Baoji to Xi'an
Not sure which was the more interesting or powerful: the Terracotta Army ...

THE REAL WAY ROUND

... or the 'tourist army' there to see it?

Linghao to Dengfeng
Shaolin Temple – stand clear!

maybe because our bikes were bigger and quicker than those the locals used, and able to travel at highway speed. Riding on the smaller state roads meant we got to see more of the country, though adding a few hours in the saddle, and often arriving in a city after dark, which is to be avoided. Trucks, cars and bikes don't have lights, and, in the dark and usual smog, head directly toward oncoming traffic. Riding for two hours or so in the pitch black, after passing an accident where a bike was in the middle of the road after being hit, its rider sitting at the side, was enough to put anyone off – it's simply too dangerous.

Reaching the secondary state roads we found these to be agricultural and just horrible. The expressways are state of the art, and the Chinese will blast through mountains to create a tunnel for one, whilst state roads have folk on their knees painting the line down the middle: a staggering contrast. And traffic on these roads is scary and random – vehicles pulling out in front of you; doing U-turns; suddenly stopping; picking up people, and whatever else they may feel like – especially when

Dunhuang
Local produce – or a car boot sale?

Baoding to Shijiazhuang
The happy face of recycling

THE REAL WAY ROUND

Baoding to Shijiazhuang
Recycling collections. No wheelie bin ghettos like those created by the UK's over-complicated rubbish collection rotas and dust carts

Kumul to Dunhuang
Cotton pickers – where was your shirt made?

China

the environment via reservoirs, dams, mining, and, I was told, even a hill built to make the wind go around the city in the opposite direction in order to blow fumes away from it. (Better to minimise the fumes I would have thought ...) This was a long day, riding for 13 hours, the last two of which in the dark. It was so tiring, and we were absolutely hammered, but a good day and very interesting.

By October we were further east, the cities getting bigger as we went. Waking one morning in Shijiazhuang (population 11m), it was so smoggy the tops of the buildings were shrouded, and barely visible. Likewise the roads where visibility was less than 20 metres (65ft) around the big cities, where drivers never put their lights on, despite it being dark, damp, grey or foggy.

Some particularly odd contrasts and anomalies were –

- State-of-the-art expressways compared to having to fill your bike from a kettle-full of petrol as bikes are not allowed on garage forecourts, because of the daft idea that the combination of an exposed engine and a fuel pump poses a high fire risk (never mind the locals smoking in a corner!)
- Towns with brand-new, brightly-coloured apartments, ten storeys high, like something akin to a new development in Manchester city centre, remained empty, compared to rural villages and valleys where the people live in overcrowded shacks
- Fridges are not switched on in any shops, so you can never have a really cold drink however hot you are from riding. They have the fridges, they just don't switch them on (hence the warm beer)
- Scenery in some areas is stunning, though marred by the presence of a massive power station
- Most people are very friendly and happy to see you, and have their photo taken, but some were really aggressive toward each other

a few stray dogs are thrown into the mix, which made us realise how lucky we'd been to date that nothing serious had occurred.

Massive tailbacks caused snarl-ups for miles, with lorries and trucks fighting for space. Filtering the bikes through the traffic and dirt tracks on the side of the road took a lot of time, energy and concentration, but had to be done to make progress. One day we were in the saddle for 11 hours, but covered just 130 miles (240km): an indication of just how busy and congested the roads were. From Pingyao to Shijiazhuang town centre roadworks necessitated riding through the centre of a building site and the actual roadworks – a new delivery of sand followed by a crater-sized hole and other excavations ten metres (32 feet) deep – in 1st gear and at 5mph was particularly challenging. To warn of roadworks ridiculous mannequins dressed in safety gear, an arm indicating the roadworks, line the road, but no one takes any notice of them, or the young girls with bright red flags doing the same thing, so a bit of a free-for-all.

Road 213 was absolutely stunning, taking us through some of the best countryside I'd seen: rice paddy fields; family-run timber yards 4000m (13,121 feet) up the mountains. The great views were scuppered a bit by reaching the top just after dusk. Coming down, the bulb of my front light blew, so I rode the two-hour descent on high beam, which, pretty uselessly, just pointed over the side of the mountain. Another huge day of riding.

We often rode past examples of how the Chinese are trying to control

Completion of the Chinese leg meant leaving the bikes at the freight terminal, and the hour-and-a-half taxi ride from Tanggu to Beijing was made particularly interesting by the fake police siren the driver used to clear the roads. Staying in Beijing whilst waiting to organise airfreight to ship the bike to Bangkok gave an opportunity to visit Tiananmen Square, the Olympic Village, Birds Nest Stadium, Cube (Olympic pool), and Forbidden City.

I have to confess to being taken in by the Tea House con, too, and this is even listed in the *Rough Guide* as one to watch out for! It works like this: we were persuaded by two delightful students, who wanted to practice their English, to go for traditional tea. This was all very nice and amicable until the bill arrived: £70 for four hot drinks! By the time we'd converted the amount and realised how much it was (and why they'd not wanted to have their photos taken), they had disappeared with the cash and we were bundled out of the tea shop (which was also in on the scam). Try and complain? All of a sudden no one speaks English ...

Wuwei to Lanzhou
Mass harvest versus simple harvest. In the country wheat is separated from chaff by laying out crops on the roads and allowing the traffic to drive over it

A final day in Tanngu to pack the bikes in a box, disconnect the batteries, drain the fuel, let the air out the tyres, and a full clean was all done in an afternoon, followed by a celebratory drink with Ron and a random Chinese family that had adopted us for the evening. A group of Chinese guys got us absolutely steaming drunk on very strong alcohol – not sure what it was but it had a bull on the front of the bottle and was 40% proof. We drank it neat and it left me with a huge hangover the next day: a great last night in China, though.

We left China on 17 October via Beijing airport: destination Bangkok. Airfreight for the bikes was organised by an agent in Tanggu – cash only with no definite date for their departure. The rest of our party had left on an earlier flight to the UK, leaving their bikes at the port as these were being seafreighted home, which takes about a month.

Before starting on the trip I'd been advised not to fly before the bike just in case it was held by Customs, but then I'd also said I would avoid riding in the dark. On a journey like this, adaptability is required.

On the bike front, before loading it I'd changed the rear pads, brake pads, oil and filter, adjusted the chain and replaced the cush drive rubbers (a sizeable job that took about three hours, as they were very worn). The

China

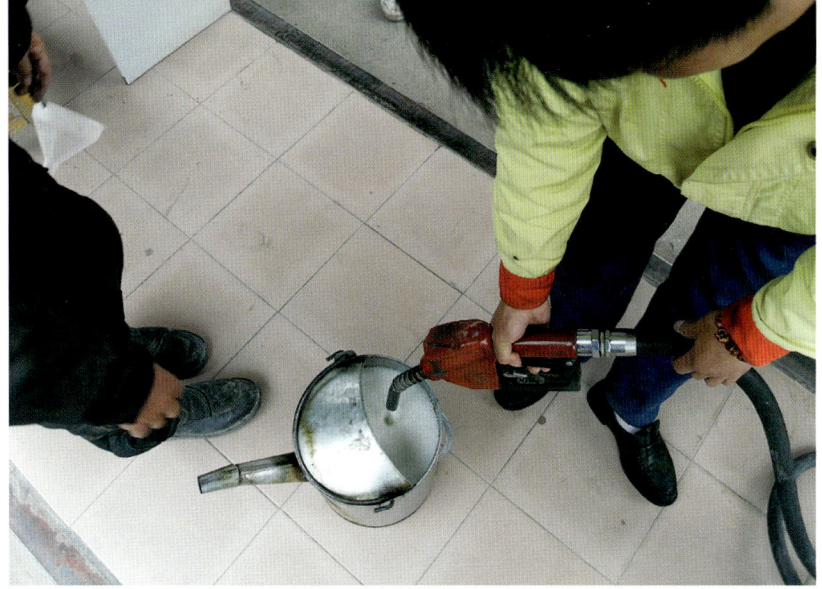

Tianjin to Tanggu
Okay, this is definitely verging on Mad Max proportions!

question was, were these correctly fitted in the first place, as it became apparent, subsequently, that this is the only real problem on early Ténérés: the rubbers soon become damaged. Despite this, the bike was performing well.

Gulja
In China, the petrol stations are massive – often with 12 pumps – always immaculate and generally new-build: that's the upside. The downside is that bikes are not alowed on to the forecourt, the reason for which, as far as I could understand, is that it's thought that heat from the exposed engine could ignite, or cause an explosion. So, how to refuel? Each station has a 5-litre kettle which you fill from the pump, walk over to your bike on the edge of the station, and fill the tank by hand using the kettle. A 5-litre kettle of fuel cost 40 yuan (around £4), and refuelling a number of bikes (given the size of our tanks) could take an hour and a half. Nuts. Has to be the first real inefficiency I experienced in China, and neither am I convinced about the sense of a motor versus the kettle process and possible fuel spillages – of which there were many

Beijing (opposite)
The Cube – recycled glass? The Olympic stadia was jaw-dropping for two reasons: 1) design brilliance 2) contrast with the villages I had passed through earlier in the week. Tiananmen Square contained the world's biggest plasma screen for the 60th Anniversary celebrations

Zhangye-Wuwei
I noticed a strong community spirit in a number of towns, particularly in Wuwei and Zhangye where kids played basketball in the parks alongside exercise machines being used by elderly people. I couldn't see this happening in England; more likely the kids would be throwing insults – and maybe even missiles – at the elderly. Generally, there's a really good feeling in all of the cities

Thailand

Dates in country	Sun 18-Fri 30 October
Number of days	13
Population (millions)	65
Capital	Bangkok
Area (km sq)	515,000
Currency	Baht
Entry/exit points	From Beijing to Bangkok (flight). Exit into Malaysia at Bukit Kayu Hitam
Total distance miles (km)/date	12,070 (19,425)/Fri 23 Oct
Average miles (km) per day	Just 45 (72) per day as spent a week in Bangkok waiting for bike to arrive
Accommodation	Mostly backpacker accommodation – one beach camp
Food	As spicy as you want it (and usually hotter than expected: stand by!)
Value	Not as good as five years ago, or so people say. Buy from street vendors and seek out local markets for real value
Rating (out of 10)	8

In a nutshell
Same-same but different. Easy to ride in and well set up for tourism – Thailand provided a relaxing break from previous three/four countries.

Rider notes
Quite wet: imminent rainy season meant wet afternoons; good roads.
Bike – Oil change at mid-point of country.
Maps – *Lonely Planet Thailand, Vietnam Road Atlas*.

Route
South on road 4 (Bang Saphan, Laem Son National Park); turned east on the 401 past Khao Sok National Park, Krabbi (Ao Nang) Hat Tham Phra Nang National Park, Phattalung (staying at Hat Chong Ke) into Malyasia via Hat Yai.

Rider log
Landed at Bangkok airport early (1am) the morning of Sunday 18 October

Bangkok (left)
Fresh pineapple served in a small, clear, plastic bag with a cocktail stick – wow! The young girl serving it had Ninja-type knife skills, and could prepare a pineapple in under ten seconds

Bang Saphan to Laem Son National Park (above)
Once again, a simple setup and talented team produced the best steamed dumplings ever tasted. The dumplings contained minced pork, water chestnuts, bamboo shoots, prawns, etc

with no plans, but headed to Khao San Road area to sort out accommodation for the next few days. Although hopeful that the bike would arrive soon, the reality was it was still in China with no confirmed date of arrival in Bangkok, despite my best efforts before leaving that country. I therefore had the luxury of a few days to hang out in Bangkok to catch up on some administration and buy any additional kit that was needed.

A good place to start in respect of the latter is the colossal Chatuchak weekend market with over 15,000 stalls. Entry to the Grand Palace (also worth a visit) was around £5, which included an English-speaking guide and a brochure: a good deal compared to China's very crowded Terracotta Army exhibit which charged £18 to get in with extra payment for a guide.

Bangkok city was interesting: always something going on and worth exploring the street vendors, smaller local markets, bars and coffee houses. District markets seem to focus on a certain type of product – one market was

Bangkok
A mixture of bustle and tranquility. Wander around one of the city's temples in complete silence and calm, then exit into the noise and hustle of the street, packed with scooters, tuk-tuks and street vendors

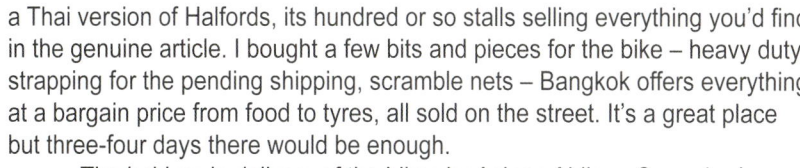
Thailand

a Thai version of Halfords, its hundred or so stalls selling everything you'd find in the genuine article. I bought a few bits and pieces for the bike – heavy duty strapping for the pending shipping, scramble nets – Bangkok offers everything at a bargain price from food to tyres, all sold on the street. It's a great place but three-four days there would be enough.

The hold-up in delivery of the bikes by Asiana Airlines Cargo had a knock-on effect, delaying, in turn, the scheduling of boats – which are limited in number and often unreliable – to take the bikes from Malaysia to Indonesia, and then to Australia. On the flip side I'd allowed six months to get to Australia, and six months in South/Central America, so even with this slight delay I was on schedule. At this stage of the trip it was just myself and Ron, planning our route to Australia: basically, get out of Bangkok and head south, then across the Indonesian Islands to Timor where the bikes could be seafreighted from Dili to Darwin.

Frustratingly, the bikes didn't arrive in Bangkok until 8.10am on Sunday 25 October – a national holiday! Despite the probability that certain departments and offices would be closed – or have only a skeleton staff (Customs, for example) at best, we went to the airport to see if we could at least make a start/find cargo offices, which can take over an hour at international airports.

Twice we were told that everything was closed, although one office had a couple of staff on overtime. Fortunately, a few phone calls were made and an agent arrived within the hour. After explaining that the bikes had come from China via Korea, forms were signed and bike paperwork exchanged (Carnet de Passage and passport were copied), plus, of course, a couple of cash payments – this was Thailand, after all, and favours cost money. Subsequently, a few offices were opened, including the 'Personal Effects and Privilege of Goods Section,' and seven individual payments (totalling £90) were made by us over the day. That may seem a lot. but crossing the border from Russia to Kazakhstan cost £60, and there were more people and effort involved at the airport, which made the 'fees' seem more reasonable. Upon my return to the UK nine months later, I had to pay a similar amount at Gatwick. I wasn't too worried about the pay-offs, in any case; it was all about getting the bikes and riding away, which we achieved by six that evening.

Leaving Bangkok during the Monday morning rush hour was fun. The South East Asia mapping from Garmin was excellent – just remember no bikes on the highway (a positive). Zigzagging through all the traffic via the small city back roads and four-lane intersections was wicked. Although busy, traffic was more organised than in China. Once out of the city we headed south toward Malaysia, and enjoyed a great day (October 26) back in the saddle, covering 256 miles (412km), taking total mileage to 12,075 (19,432km). To top it off the day ended with a great rough camp at Bang Saphan on a lovely beach near a couple of local fishing families.

Riding in Thailand was superb as the roads are incredible, and the people extremely friendly. We experienced a few very heavy downpours – so heavy on one occasion that the bike side stand sank into the softened ground to the point that it went over. The rain can be so hard that it simply washes away the ground.

A further 150 miles (241km) (total 12,700 miles/20,438km) took us to Hat Chong Ke about 200 miles (322km) north of the Malaysian border. Hat Chong Ke has wet lands on the edge of Lake Phatthalung inside the coast line north of Songkhla, with bright green rice paddies. I loved all the farming

cnt'd page 77

Bangkok

Goods in – receiving the bike at Bangkok airport – happy days

Pit stop – finding a garage to complete an oil change was easy. The course I did at Wakefield College was good, but more often than not locals wanted to carry out all tasks, which was fair enough. After all, I've never been to Kwik Fit and changed my own car tyres, and these guys were experts who had probably been doing oil changes since a young age. It's important to keep an open mind

Bangkok
A stitch in time ... Another country – and a recurring theme in all countries since Kazakhstan – where repairing what you own is the norm, rather than replacement

Bang Saphan to Laem Son National Park
On the road lots of things grab your attention. The camels in Kazakhstan were impressive, but elephants working in the Thai mountains were simply awesome. Meet Bunsong the elephant (translates to 'good deed sent')

THE REAL WAY ROUND

Bang Saphan to Laem Son National Park
Travel and transportation, Thai-style

Hat Chong Ke
Hard-working, wonderful people toil in the rice fields at Hat Chong Ke

stuff in Romania and this was just as good: farming; water buffalo; fishing. Breakfast the next day at the side of the road was rice, egg and some pork – 'same-same but different' as an English breakfast really. In remote farming areas images and photos of the King are commonplace; there appears to be huge respect for the Royal Family country-wide. The King overseas the development of rural areas in terms of building roads and other infrastructure; his people appear to idolise him.

Heading toward the border we rode through a Muslim area (Sadao), noticeable for the women wearing headscarves. Despite reported tension on the east side of the border we experienced only friendliness. The border crossing into Malaysia was smooth and took just an hour-and-a-half: passports; bags; bikes. The Carnet de Passage was used properly for the first time – sections retained and stamped – whereas in Thailand all of it had been photocopied.

Malaysia

Dates in country	Sat 31 Oct-Thur 5 Nov
Number of days	6
Population (millions)	25
Capital	Kuala Lumpur
Area (km sq)	330,000
Currency	Ringgit
Entry/exit points	From Thailand at Dan Nok. Exit into Indonesia at Medan from George Town
Total distance miles (km)/date	12,700 (20,439)/Fri 30 Oct
Average miles (km) per day	100 (160)
Accommodation	Backpacker hostels
Food	Indian; strawberries, honey. Tea from the Cameron Highlands
Value	Lots of tourism so not the cheapest but excellent quality
Rating (out of 10)	8

Local media reported heavy rain

In a nutshell
Great roads; fabulous walking and riding amongst tea plantations in the Cameron Highlands. Orang Asli village was interesting.

Route
Kedah, Ipoh, Cameron Highlands, Butterworth, George Town, Penang.

Rider notes
Bike – Good to see other big bikes on the road. The highways are set up for bikes, but beware mudslides.
Maps – Free tourist map.

Rider log
First stop in Malaysia was Sungai Petani: no tolls for bikes so a straight blast down the freeway and a relaxing evening at the end. From Sungai Petani it was straight down the highway and then left on Road 181

Malaysia

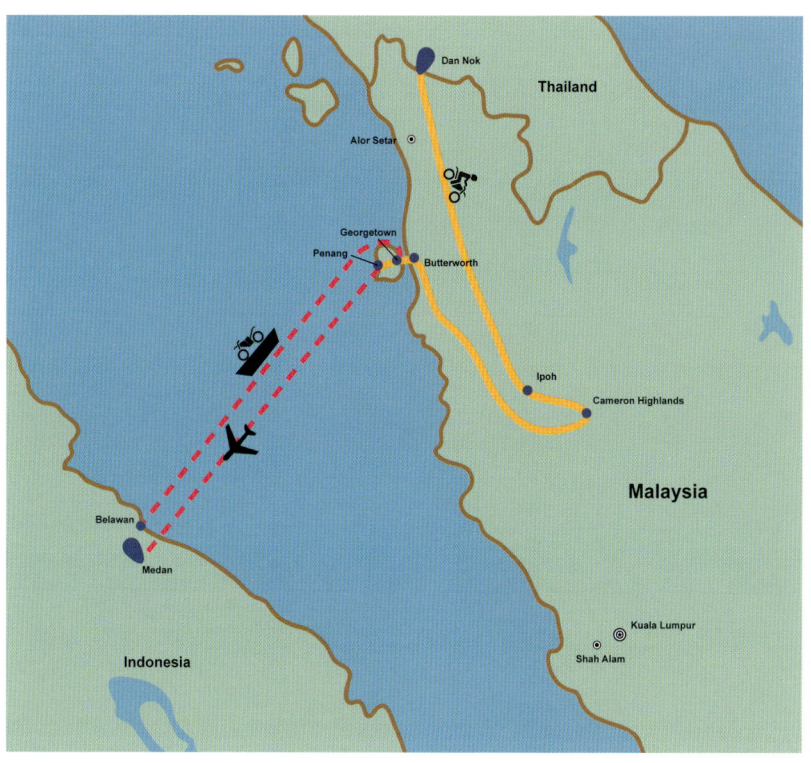

(one of the best yet) to the Cameron Highlands, with an absolutely stunning, winding road up into the mountains, through tea plantations and jungle. Obviously a well-ridden road as a number of sports bikes were also ripping up and down the mountain. Ron went to Kuala Lumpur to see relatives, which gave me a couple of days to hang out in the Cameron Highlands and enjoy some comfort amongst the tourists. All of a sudden there were reminders of the UK: kids listening to the Arctic Monkeys; three-pin plug sockets, and great Indian food.

Exactly three months into the trip (which had gone by really quickly) the mileage to Malaysia was 12,926 (20,801km).

It was very wet, and newspapers were headlining the monsoon and mudslides that took out two cars on the road to the highlands. The rain was that heavy it caused landslides.

The plentiful backpackers in the Cameron Highlands meant good facilities, allowing some route planning and emails to Northern Territory Motorcycles in Darwin, Australia, to arrange a big service for the bike. Whilst on the road, in order to maintain momentum and enjoy good riding, its important to think about the next week's route planning and timings, whilst keeping an eye on a three-month plan to order necessary parts and arrange servicing in advance. The Yamaha Ténéré had only just arrived in Australia, so parts for it would definitely not be in stock there.

Our relaxing trek through plantations and jungle came to an abrupt end in an effort to make an appointment with Mr Lim of Cakra Shipping in Georgetown (a ride named the 'Penang Dash' by Ron). Mr Lim was the agent who organised for the bikes to set sail that very night (Wednesday 4 November), arriving next day at the port of Belawan, Sumatra, Indonesia, after an 18-hour, freight-only crossing, necessitating a flight for us from Penang to Medan.

Parit Buntar to Cameron Highlands
Fresh chickenburger, please! Matchday special – Man Utd is the biggest brand in the world – official merchandise only: Old Trafford burgers?

THE REAL WAY ROUND

Cameron Highlands
Father's Lodge – an old military bunker – which charged only about 30 ringgits (£6) per night): a really cool place. Like a green carpet rolling across the hillsides and valleys, tea plantations are everywhere. Harvesting is automated, using massive cutting blades (strimmers), and a hoover-style bag attachment which cuts across the top of the bushes, taking off the top leaves. It's farming on a mass scale, but, later on in Indonesia, I witnessed an army of workers completing the same job by hand

Malaysia

At this point I opted for a two-month visa for Indonesia, which required another application, compared to a one-month visa that was provided on arrival. Ron went for the one-month version, and raced to Sydney for New Year – cheerio, Ron, see you back in the UK; ride safe. A recent earthquake and the pending rainy season persuaded me to go for the two-month tourist visa and go at a slower pace.

The previously mentioned 'Penang Dash' – plus a visa application and a race from Medan to Belawan on the back of a crazy bike taxi to collect the Ténéré before the port office shut on a Friday afternoon – went something like this –

Wednesday 4 November
- Cameron Highlands to Georgetown, Pulau Pinang (170 miles/273km; crossed the impressive Penang Bridge) to complete shipping documents with Mr Lim
- Georgetown to Butterworth Port to put bikes on the boat (loaded with cans of Carlsberg – will they make it? 'Probably')
- Find digs in Georgetown (£3.50 per night – bargain!)

Cameron Highlands to Georgetown
Shipping from Penang to Belawan Port, Indonesia. The captain put me in mind of Popeye, although the boat was full of cans of Carlsberg rather than spinach!

THE REAL WAY ROUND

Thursday 5 November
- Visit agent to get 60-day visa, only to discover a flight booking to Indonesia is required first
- Flight ticket booked, 530 ringgits (£114: expensive, but last-minute and only few seats left)
- Make visa application at agents but refused as one-way flight and no proof of onward journey
- Make trip by bus to the Indonesian Embassy; visa passport photo refused on the basis it wasn't on a red background. Find photo kiosk, get photos and return to Embassy
- Explain the one-way ticket, pay 170 ringgits (£36) and submit the application (it's an overnight process)

Friday 6 November
- Check out of hostel
- Collect 60-day visa from Embassy (only available after midday). Successful, despite not having an Indonesian sponsor
- Get to airport – using taxi not bus. Relax at airport with a deep breath and coffee
- Fly at 3pm from Penang to Medan (the clocks go back an hour – critical bonus)
- Fifty minute, white-knuckle bike taxi from Medan to Belawan – random address from Mr Lim; not the port – 150,000 Indonesian rupiah (£10). (I'd been told by a taxi driver that this journey would take an hour-and-a-half so lots of time saved)
- Get from the agent's office to the port
- Paperwork stamped at port warehouse, 750,000 Indonesian rupiah (£51) payment, bike collected!

I had to get to the customs office before it closed at 5pm for the weekend to avoid the bike being stored until Monday morning. It was a rush – especially adding in the language problems and the need for another currency – but worth it. The longer a bike and kit is warehoused the greater the chance it will be tampered with or, even worse, disappear, plus, it was better not to have to over-weekend in a port town. I'd already spent over a million rupiah – hold on, that's only about £69! By 6.30 that evening I had the bike up and running and accommodation sorted: time to eat and do some route planning.

Total mileage for the trip 13,276 (21,365km); total mileage for the bike 20,000 (32,186km), and in good spirits (touch wood).

Indonesia

Dates in country	Fri 6 Nov-Tue 15 Dec
Number of days	40
Population (millions)	247
Capital	Jakarta
Area (km sq)	1,950,000 (up to 17,000 islands)
Currency	Rupiah
Entry/exit points	From Malaysia into Belawan/Medan, Sumatra. Exit into Timor-Leste at Batugade
Total distance miles (km)/date	16,680 (26,844)/Fri 11 Dec
Average miles (km) per day	180 (290: two decent breaks at 60 (96) and 120 (193) miles: seems low mileage but entailed 8-10 hours' riding
Accommodation	100% hostels/hotels. Amazing value: a single room with shower, toilet, and balcony overlooking the lakes was just 50,000 rupiah (less than £3.50)
Food	Pisang Rai: essentially, bananas and coconut wrapped in a rice sheet and some kind of coffee. Sumatra has the most gorgeous coffee, plus excellent grilled chicken
Value	Some of the lowest-priced fuel and accommodation encountered
Rating (out of 10)	10: Indonesia exceeds expectations in every possible way

In a nutshell

Rice fields; wooden huts on the outskirts of towns; bustling towns; moped shops; small street food stalls known locally as kaki limas selling amazingly tasty fresh food (great whilst on the road); volcanoes; telephone card upgrades; waving fruit sellers; people driving with their right indicator on, warning of a pending overtake manoeuvre (and they do).

Handwritten signs: 'Hati Hati' ('Danger Danger') is commonplace (always in red), before the road turns to mush; mud cobbles; stones and

THE REAL WAY ROUND

Belawan Port
Sumatran welcome to Indonesia. What a reception in Belawan, whilst sorting the paperwork in order to collect the bike

Muara Bungo to Lubuklinggau
Sumatran durian fruit – big and spiky on the outside; soft, white and fleshy on the inside, and, man, did it smell (so bad it was banned from hotels). Hugely popular, it's usually eaten in segments but I thought it tasted bloody awful. Locals spend ages selecting their durian: sniffing, squeezing and shaking it like the most expert wine tasters. I never discovered my wine nose, though – luckily for me – lots of other fruit was available

Indonesia

intense roadworks, complete with a few mad bus drivers honking their horns; people shouting "Hey mister, hey mister," excited to see a foreigner.

Route
Sumatra, Java, Bali, Lombok, Sumbawa, Flores, West Timor (seven islands – be prepared for lots of ferry crossings).

Rider notes
Journey times should be doubled: if a local says it will take 20 minutes, allow at least 40! I learnt this on day one in Indonesia after being told it would take 30 minutes to ride through Medan (it actually took an hour), as no bikes are allowed on the highway that bypasses the city. This reminded me of China: poor road surface and traffic heading in all directions. Road surfaces, generally, are poor, with landslides (muddy surface) and large cracks caused by recent earthquake (Sumatra). A 50-mile (80km) journey can take two hours.

Heavy, monsoon-like rain usually starts in the afternoon (3-4pm), and continues for long periods.

Bike – It became necessary to make an adjustment to my bike trousers by cutting additional vents into each leg at the inside top thigh to increase air flow to family jewels.

Maps – *Nelles Maps Indonesia* (bought in Thailand for 225 baht (£5)).

Rider log
Indonesia equalled or surpassed the rest of Asia in many respects: the scenery is prettier than the Cameron Highlands; great people in cities and villages; the lovely coastlines and beaches; the hustle and bustle and specific sites of interest. However, Indonesia does not seem at all organised or prepared for tourism for some unknown reason (Bali being the exception to this).

Sumatra
Route: Belawan, Medan, Samosir Island (via Tuk Tuk), Padang Sidempuan, Bukittinggi, Muara Bungo, Lubuklinggau, Baturaja to Bandar Lampung.

The food in Indonesia is sensational, and a bit of everything is usually served: a big bowl of rice and spicy chicken; ordinary chicken; beef; liver; hard-boiled eggs; vegetables – each served in twos in their own little dishes.

I left Bukittinggi at 7.30am after rising at 6.30. Although it's cool this time in the morning, with all my kit on, I was absolutely drenched in sweat

THE REAL WAY ROUND

Samosir Island
Sumatran food rules. There are lots of places to eat along the roadside: choose the busiest to get the best food and most banter

before I even set off. As my gear was still wet from the four-hour monsoon I had ridden through the previous evening, it felt just like being in a sauna. Manoeuvring the bike from its hidden storage area was difficult and hard work. It's so heavy, and pulling and pushing it takes some effort, so a sweaty start to the day for me. Once riding, however, with some airflow, it was fine.

My journey was about 180 miles (289km) (total mileage just over 14,000/22,530km). I'd splashed out a bit as the hotel was around £15, and actually quite nice, with WiFi so I was able to download photos, audio (diary), and use Skype. My first hotel had cost £3, the next rising to £9 and now £15, so I needed to watch the budget, and get the next one down to £5 or thereabouts. Distances between sizable towns were in the region of 186 miles (300km), and great scenery, farming, and mountains (complete with bandits) lined the route. Generally, it took around nine hours to cover 186 miles (300km), given a clear run with a few breaks. En route I saw someone selling guns, which felt a little strange, despite seeing quite a lot of guns (on a daily basis, actually). The gun-seller had five or six weapons, one of which a chap standing next to him was checking out; looking down the barrel. The guns were quite openly being sold in the street: should I be worried about that, I wondered ...?

I rode past Lake Singkarak, then through a small town called Solok, complete with crater lakes and volcanoes, just sensational with volcanic mounds everywhere. The rice paddy fields were home to big volcanic rocks and looked fantastic. I didn't stop to take photos as it was throwing it down with rain, but what fantastic sights.

Indonesia

Lubuklinggau to Baturaja
Sumatran brick production, Indonesian-style. A small, family business makes bricks by hand, firing them in a wood-burning oven

I eventually arrived at Muara Bungo, which is slap bang in the middle of Sumartra. It's home to quite a few wild monkeys, which lie and sit at the side of the road, dashing off into the forest as you approach.

I got myself into a bit of a situation en route to Padang Sidempuan when I came across two bikers who waved me down. I stopped for a chat/photos (nothing new in that) but, unbeknownst to me, they called friends, members of the same biking community, who joined us to welcome me to the town. Invited to their house I regretted accepting almost instantly as the atmosphere became odd when the numbers swelled to ten lads and a big truck appeared outside. Only one of the men spoke good English, and some of the others seemed decidedly twitchy. The garage where my bike was contained scales, sacks, handcuffs, and a fake gun. I was uncomfortable and, for the first time, texted my location to the UK just in case I should disappear – not a nice thought. It's possible I misread the situation but it didn't feel right,

Samosir Island
Sumatran love. Water buffalo are prized possessions

Samosir Island to Padang Sidempuan
Ride safe – go steady: landslides and large cracks in the roads are commonplace following heavy rains and earthquakes

especially after seeing bike luggage that was obviously too big for an Indonesian moped, and persistent questioning about the value of my bike. I knew I had to leave.

I had a response to my text, and made up some nonsense about it being from a friend who was also riding and had now arrived in town. Quickly, I got my stuff together and left. The lesson here is, if invited to go anywhere with somebody, only do so after arranging accommodation so you have somewhere to go to if things get weird – and trust your instinct.

The following day a bus went over the side of the mountain. Every window was smashed, and the 20 or so survivors who had managed to scramble up the bank were crouched at the side of the road looking down at the wreckage. Bus drivers do long shifts, the roads are poor, and the vehicles are hammered: a worrying combination.

One sight that really caught my eye was an attractive, middle-aged lady walking down the road with a shotgun on her shoulder. Whilst not uncommon to see guns this was a striking combo (I wish I had got a photo ...).

Java

Route: Tangerang, Bandung (avoid Jakarta), Kutoarjo Borobudur Temple (UNESCO world heritage site), Solo, Mt Bromo.

Dropping out of the mountains the

Indonesia

Belawan Port
Sumatran taxi and rank

Munduk
Balinese Wonder Woman

Lubahanbajo to Bajawa
Flores Wonder Woman

Samosir Island to Padang Sidempuan
Sumatran Wonder Woman

Bandung to Kutoajaro
Javanese Wonder Woman

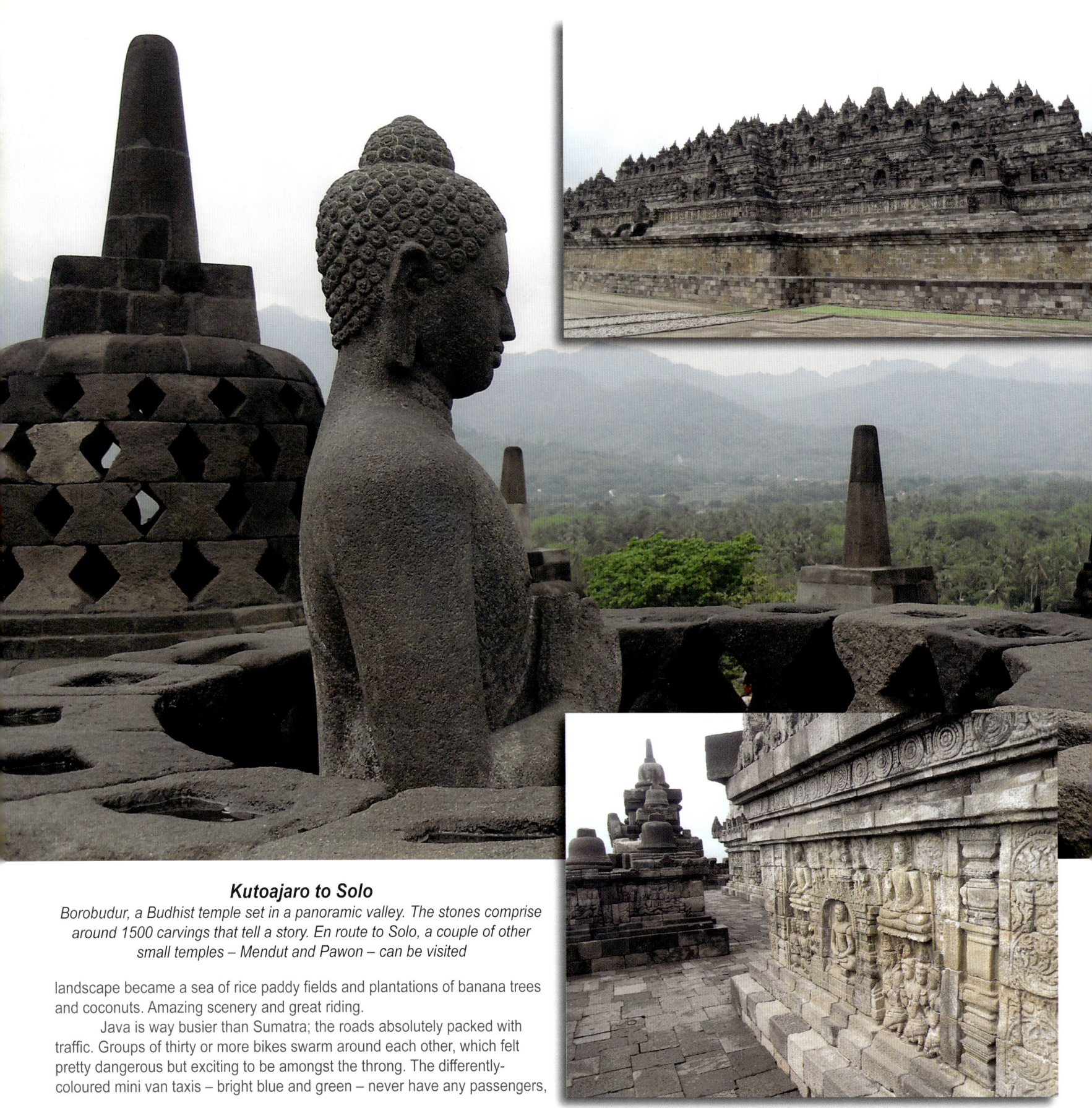

Kutoajaro to Solo
Borobudur, a Budhist temple set in a panoramic valley. The stones comprise around 1500 carvings that tell a story. En route to Solo, a couple of other small temples – Mendut and Pawon – can be visited

landscape became a sea of rice paddy fields and plantations of banana trees and coconuts. Amazing scenery and great riding.

Java is way busier than Sumatra; the roads absolutely packed with traffic. Groups of thirty or more bikes swarm around each other, which felt pretty dangerous but exciting to be amongst the throng. The differently-coloured mini van taxis – bright blue and green – never have any passengers,

Indonesia

Kutoajaro to Solo
Javan 'freight terminal'

but crawl up and down the road touting for clients, causing massive congestion. The opposite end of the scale is the mini van that should carry about eight passengers, but which struggles with double the recommended capacity. Whilst riding, I got way too much attention from people/other vehicles within touching distance, even, on some occasions, contact at slow speed.

Going through a town earlier that week I came across a street party. Car and bike tyres had been laid along the road to slow/stop traffic, the villagers' version of speed humps.

Roads were bloody hectic, and I hoped that, once past Jakarta and off the main busy stretch, they would be calmer. Weirdly, by way of indicating direction, people flapped their arms like a bird, and lots of vans didn't have rear lights or indicators. Bike riders just frantically waved their hands, which can mean different things in different situations: 'I'm stopping/turning/moving over.' All a bit of a guessing game, so generally best to stay clear.

The following morning I got out the city and onto mountain roads (twists and hairpins, fabulous roads) quickly. Again, the scenery was amazing: I know I keep saying this, but there were all different kinds of farming at different stages of the journey, and further along there might be an area that was being harvested, or the fields could be flooded (paddy fields are constantly being turned over so that no time is wasted, or area untended).

Torrential rain in the afternoon caused me to stop for shelter and coffee in a Dunkin' Donuts (which I didn't expect to find), watching as the road turned into a river, with bottles and debris bobbing in it. The locals got busy taking off layers of clothing as I was donning waterproofs to keep my kit dry. Stopped at traffic lights they were shedding shoes, rolling up trouser legs and getting down to a t-shirt – almost riding around in their underpants – which made sense, I guess. Why get yourself and your clothes wet when you could take off the clothes and keep them dry in a bag?

To get to Mount Bromo from Solo (which is 240 miles (386km)) I'd made a list of twelve towns to ride through/look out for in order to stay on track – depart Solo; Sragen; Madiun; Caruban; Kertosono; Mojokerto; Sidoarjo; Bangil; Pasuruan; Probolinggo; Sukopura; Cemoro Lawang – the list lying on the top of my tank bag. Pushing through these places, trying to find the next sign, was almost impossible but great fun, each day riding through the hectic towns and stunning countryside of Indonesia.

Bali (amazing Bali!)
Route: Gilimanuk, Seminyak, Danau Batur volcanic crater lake, Munduk,

Kedisan
Catch of the day

Munduk
Truly marvellous rice terraces

Lovina (north coast), Amed (east coast), and Padangbai (ferry port to Lombok Island).

Bali attracts lots of tourists, so facilities and food with a few western-style treats are easy to come by, quite refreshing, and make a trip round the island very enjoyable: highly recommended.

Caught the 1pm ferry to Bali which docks in Gilimanuk, north-west of the island (mileage 15,622/25,141km), followed by a good ride along the south coast to Seminyak, where I was greeted by a power cut – electricity is turned off overnight every week in one town on the island to save energy.

A few things had begun to worry me about the bike at this stage. 1) It was generally not running smoothly, was in need of a service, and sometimes cut out as not idling at the correct speed, requiring a little throttle when stationary (it had even cut out when changing down). 2) After 15,622 miles (25,141km), the back tyre was on its last legs. The bike was way over the recommended mileage on both, but I hoped they would get me to Australia if I could just hop over these final islands. 3) Most importantly the horn had stopped working properly (probably through over-use): muffled and about half as loud as it should be.

Bali has one striking difference to the rest of Indonesia: the island religion is Hindu as opposed to Muslim. It is also tourist-friendly (and hugely popular with Australians), so I pottered around the island's beaches (Seminyak, Lovina and Lipah); volcanic lakes (Danau Batur), and amazing countryside and farming villages, with shimmering rice paddy fields near Munduk. Temperatures were extremely high, topping at 39°C – if stuck in traffic with the engine running the heat is incredible.

In and around National Parks the roads are as unpredictable as those on the other islands, and one of the most dangerous things is how fast the

buses go, and their drivers' expectation that everyone and everything will shift out of the way. One guy was riding a bike, on the back of which was a wicker basket, containing what looked like toilet rolls, to be honest, packed high and wide. As the bus passed the biker, it clipped one side of the basket, causing the rider to wiggle all over the road; goodness knows how he didn't lose it completely. The bike riders are amazing. I followed a girl across the east end of Java to the port, and she was so quick, she knew every little bump in the road. Her bike could have only been a 125cc, and all she had on was flip-flops, jeans and a t-shirt. The only concession they seem to make is to wear their jackets back to front to provide extra protection against the wind – and that's it.

After a couple of days in Amed – which were very nice – I got the ferry from Bali to to Lombok.

Lombok and Sumbawa
Route: Lombok (Lembar to Wanasabe) and Sumbawa (Alas to Sape).

The ferry crossing to Lombok on Friday 4 December (16,000 miles/25,749km) took around five hours. The ticket office at the ferry tried

cnt'd page 96

Indonesia

Lubuklinggau to Baturaja
Shimmering rice fields and workers: riding through these areas was an absolute treat

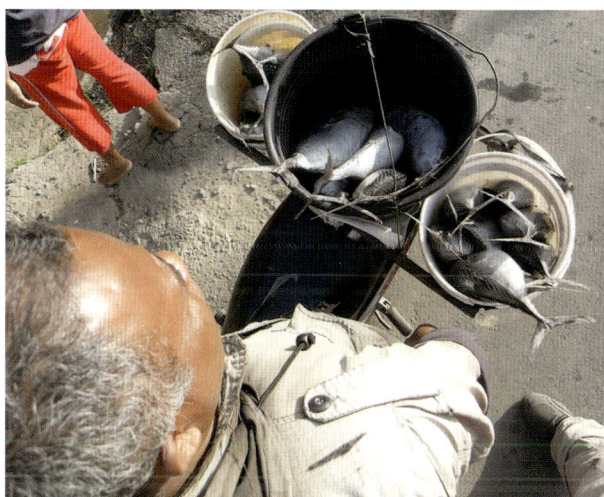

Bukittinggi to Muara Bungo
Bike modifications were rife, and, in the main, personal adaptions enabled owners to carry out work tasks

Refuelling
'Please pay before refuelling' is definitely the rule in remote areas (if you can find someone to take control of the guard dog!). At major stations pumps are specified for mopeds and cars. Because so many people ride mopeds, though, the queues for these pumps are massive. Unfortunately, the Ténéré fell into the moped/bike category, which meant queueing with twenty or so others in the baking heat, even though the car pump was free (the people behind me couldn't believe how long it took to fill the Ténéré's 23-litre tank), and it was often quicker to refuel at the local entrepreneur's garage, using the 2 or 3 litre bottles on sale there

to charge me extra for the Yamaha as it was bigger than the bikes it usually carried, I managed to persuade them it was a moped on the basis it was a single cylinder, and it cost 78,000 Indonesian rupiah (£5) for the crossing.

It was dark when the ferry docked, which always makes riding more hazardous – simply picking out the road is almost impossible as there are no street lights – and, as I'd met a guy on the ferry who was also heading toward Mataram, I followed him. The locals know every pothole and surface change, and slalom through these obstacles with such ease it's difficult to keep up with their smaller, nimbler machines.

The first three hotels I tried in Lombok were full (this hadn't happened before, though it was later than usual) but, luckily, I found a great simple little place called Oka Homestay. Lombok is very similar to Bali with its paddy fields and huge, volcanic mountain in the middle. After a quick overnight stop I was keen to make up some time, so headed east toward the ferry port for the two-and-a-half hour crossing to the island of Sumbawa.

Sumbawa is a very poor island which (as far as I could see) produces salt as its main industry. It does have some very nice bays, mountains, and lots of farming. The main bay is called Saleh Bay and makes a great coastal run of dodging monkeys in the mountains, goats and cows in farming areas, and decent road conditions with the exception of village approaches where overuse has eroded the tarmac and resulted in ruts. One guy came off his bike right in front of me after catching the wheels in a linear rut: once in a rut, it's very hard to get out of it, but the traffic is so hectic that it's hard to slow down anyway. This time he got it wrong and he and the bike flipped over, hitting the road pretty hard. Note to self: take it very steady – I was always

Indonesia

Flores bling

A favourite pastime seems to be blinging-up vehicles. Mini van buses are something else; usually driven aggressively and decked out like sponsored sports cars with stickers. The front usually has a massive sticker designed to minimise sun glare, and sometimes one at the bottom, too, the driver peeking through a horizontal, 3-inch slit. The windscreen of one creative individual was designed like sunglasses, the driver peering out of the 'lenses.' And it didn't stop with mini vans, either: a bike in Laruntuka had switched nationalities and become a British Yamaha in Indonesia. They love superbikes here, and everyone knows who Valentino Rossi is. I stopped in the smallest of villages where a woman pointed at the Yamaha logo on my bike and said "Valentino Rossi." Rossi's obviously bigger than Man United, even (and so he should be)

THE REAL WAY ROUND

Sumbawa-Besar to Sape
Sumbawa fishing village

Bajawa to Moni
Flores Kelimutu National Park: three coloured lakes in volcanic craters

acutely aware that an incident like that could easily bring my trip to an abrupt and unexpected end.

The midway point on the island was Sumbawa-Besar, a good location to overnight, as I met so many friendly people. The town is run-down but the people were amazing. Loads and loads of ponies with traps waited in bays for passengers like London taxis – one-horsepower travel. Unfortunately, the lodge where I stayed was so filthy that I set up my own mobile bathroom using bits of kit such as my foldaway Ortlieb camping sink. I spotted ants running across the bed and thought "thank goodness for my sleeping liner." The lack of power and a very noisy generator right outside my room made for a very hot, humid, noisy and dirty night - but I was still smiling!

Sape, the village I next visited at the eastern side of Sumbawa, comprised brightly-painted fishing huts on stilts at the edge of the water, a population of 50,000, and very little money or trade, so very poor. Sape itself was a lovely place, with great people, despite its rather bad write-up in the Lonely Planet guide. The hostel where I stayed charged 150,000 rupiah (just under £10), and was right near the ferry port. Deciding on an early night I boarded the ferry first thing the next morning, only to wait for three hours whilst it refuelled.

Flores
Route: Labuhanbajo, Bajawa, Ende, Larantuka.

Flores (mileage 16,335) is a mini version of Sumatra, with a road that cuts horizontally through it. It has a number of points of interest worth visiting: Rinca Island (home of the Komodo Dragon); local villages near Bajawa, and Kelimutu National Park (volcanic crater/turquoise lakes). What an island!

As previously mentioned, Rinca Island is home to the Komodo Dragon, as well as other interesting wildlife, and, whilst visiting, a BBC film crew filmed part of a documentary about dinosaurs (were they social animals?), using the Komodo Dragon as an example.

Long stretches of beach – of both black and white sand – rivalled volcanoes, palm trees and rain forests in their impressiveness. Road surfaces were fine, generally, though there's quite a bit of gravel around corners (being fussy). Catholicism is the religion here, so there are churches everywhere; mini vans (buses) are crammed full of passengers (I saw three people on a front seat designed for one, whilst still more people hung off the back). I'm not sure why I was surprised by this, given that a family of five on a moped was a common sight.

A trip to Ende was necessary in order to determine when the ferries ran to Timor. The information I received was sketchy, to say the least, as

Indonesia

Seminyak beach • Lovina beach
Stunning scenery was the norm

THE REAL WAY ROUND

Bajawa *(above & opposite, right)* • ***Kupang to Kefamenanu*** *(below)* • ***Kefamenanu Batugade*** *(opposite, left)*
Traditional villages were immaculately kept, and the people very friendly. Bajawa felt a little contrived (though still interesting) with a number of tourists evident.
The further east I rode, more authentic villages would spring up along the route

Indonesia

there's no set timetable. There were two ferry companies (I think – still not sure): Indonesian Ferries (government owned), and ASDP, but details about both were very vague. The guy at the backpacker lodge where I was staying said there would be a ferry in the morning, but the following day I arrived to discover that none was due for a week. However, a ferry crossing to Timor was scheduled from Larantuka a day's ride away. Arriving at Larantuka Saturday 12 December (16,862 miles/27,136km) I found the ferry office to be like a building site, with staff present only on those days when crossings were scheduled.

West Timor

Route: Kupang, Soe, Kefamenanu, Batugade (border with Timor Leste).

Finally made it to West Timor after an horrific ferry crossing that was due to depart Laruntuka on Monday at 10am, but eventually did so at two that afternoon. I'd already learnt that things don't happen quickly, so wasn't too surprised. Onboard the ferry loads of people were sleeping on the floor, and a huge, squealing pig was dragged on by her ears, understandably going nuts at this treatment. The poor creature was lashed to the side of the boat near my bike. Honestly, nobody would opt to travel this way, given the choice. After a cramped, 20-hour crossing the ferry docked in Kupang at six the next morning.

Disembarking, I stopped at a cafe to await the opening of the petrol station opposite, as I needed fuel. The guy in the cafe was frying up chicken for lunchtime, and I ended up having unlimited rice and fried chicken at 6.45 in the morning which, after the journey I'd just had, tasted excellent and really hit the spot.

At Kefamenanu, mileage for the trip passed the 17,000 (27,358km) mark – and on one set of tyres (which now desperately needed replacing). The engine cutting out had become more frequent: the Ténéré was definitely ready for that service in Darwin. Two vessels go to Darwin from Dili (freight only), so I needed a flight. There was one on December 20 and another three days later, but my preference was the earlier one. Having already organised/negotiated one crossing, the ferry from Flores to West Timor, three different ports, two cancellations and a 20-hour crossing to Kupang, next on the list was getting from Timor-Leste to Darwin.

Even on the poor islands I visited I found that the kids were always very clean and well presented, which made me wonder how on earth their mums got school shirts, etc, so clean by washing them in a stream? It was really nice to see some actual villages where people live and work. A woman dragging a barrow containing about ten 5lt jerry cans of water was quite a sight. The other thing you get to see is the kids (usually five to ten years of age) leaving school in a line, each with their own 5/10lt bottle or bucket that they fill at the water pump before carrying it home for their family. It's quite humbling, and makes life in the UK seem relatively easy in comparison. The villagers take such pride in their homes, the walkways around them are so clean, and you can see where they have been swept. Very primitive dwellings but always immaculate.

All the islands are quite different, West Timor noticeably so for the military presence on the move and training camps along the road. About every fifth moped had a camouflage-attired rider.

Ferry crossings

Indonesia to Timor-Leste can involve at least six ferry crossings, depending on route chosen. I didn't have time to get to Sulawesi; one of a few islands that is also worth visiting. The route I took is detailed in the table on page 104.

The bigger port towns are industrial, very busy, and quite rough – you don't want to be hanging around them for too many nights – and there are better places to spend time in any case.

cnt'd page 105

THE REAL WAY ROUND

Kefamenanu Batugade (above) • ***Muara Bungo to Lubuklinggau*** (right) • ***Kupang to Kefamenanu*** (far right)
Inquisitive village kids

Muara Bungo to Lubuklinggau (top & far left)
• **Bandung to Kutoajaro** (above, left)
• **Lubahanbajo to Bajawa** (left)
• **Kupang to Kefamenanu** (above, right)

There's lots to take in along the roadside: traffic is heavy in towns and cities; individuals collect change to build mosques; signs are difficult to interpret; food stalls line the roads, and everyday items such as newspapers are touted by sellers

THE REAL WAY ROUND

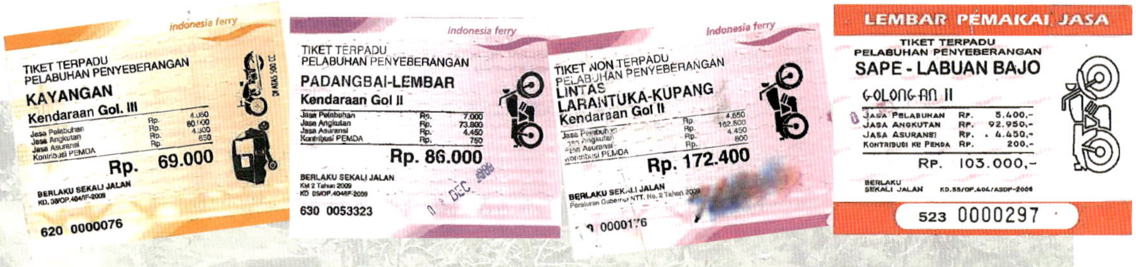

From	To	Frequency	Duration	Cost (rupiah/pounds)
Sumatra, Bakauheuni	Java, Merak	Every Hour	1 hour	69,000/4.50
Java, Banyuwangi	Bali, Gilimanuk	Every Hour	1 hour	27,000/1.75
Bali, Padang Bai	Lombok, Lembar	Every 2 hours	5 hours	86,000/5.60
Lombok, Labuhan	Sumbawa, Alas	Every 5 hours	3 hours	75,000/4.90
Sumbawa, Sape	Flores, Laubahanbajo	Once daily	7 hours	103,000/7.01
Flores, Larantuka	West Timor, Kupang	Every 4-5 hours	20 hours	172,400/11.20

Bandar Lampung to Nelayan (this page)
• **Mataram to Labuan** (opposite, top right)
• **Larantuka** (opposite, rest)
Ferry crossings. Once past the nerves and scrummage of embarkation, the actual crossings were quite relaxing, despite some passengers oinking their way across

Indonesia

The ferries are simple roll-on-roll-off vehicles, and generally old rust-buckets packed to the rafters with cars, mopeds, wagons, people and animals. Somewhat disconcertingly the wagons sway and move with the ferry, and all vehicles are chocked to compensate for their dodgy brakes. My bike was usually tethered to the side with two pieces of rope.

Getting on is difficult and risky, via small tracks, gangways, rusty wet ramps covered in rubbish, and holes and cracks everywhere: no problem in a car or wagon but potentially lethal on a big bike. The ramps rarely adjoin the gangway properly, and big gaps are filled with various items (often a large rope).

On board goods are freely traded (watches, tea and coffee, food), and mats are rented out (space to sleep, essentially). A television in a corner is usually blasting out an Indonesian film, unnoticed by those on the floor playing draughts or cards – the majority of passengers appear to sleep.

The many reports on the internet about Indonesian ferries sinking or catching fire come as no surprise, given these conditions. A ferry crossing is certainly not a pleasure cruise but it is real life, so enjoy.

Timor-Leste

Dates in country	Wed 16-Thur 17 Dec
Number of days	2
Population (millions)	1
Capital	Dili
Area (km sq)	15,000
Currency	US dollar
Entry/exit points	From Indonesia at Batugade. Exit Dili to Darwin, Australia
Total distance miles (km)/date	17,160 (27,616)/Fri 18 Dec
Average miles (km) per day	100 (160)
Accommodation	Hostel
Food	Mostly American/Australian influence in Dili
Value	Average
Rating (out of 10)	7: UN presence in Dili is over-the-top

In a nutshell
Fabulous villages; Dili interesting with simple museum.

Route
Batugade to Dili.

Rider notes
Bike – Intriguing villages; road surface very hit and miss
Map – *Nelles Maps Indonesia*.

Rider log
Completed the border crossing at Batugade in an hour, where the bike and the kit – both panniers and the soft bag – were thoroughly investigated (most items removed and checked over); the only time this was done on the entire trip. The Customs chaps made a complete mess of the Carnet de Passage, taking all sections of the docket (it's fair to say that very few officers know what the Carnet is about), although I did manage to retrieve the docket as the next stage of the trip entails shipment via an agency, which required all the paperwork to be in place.

Timor-Leste

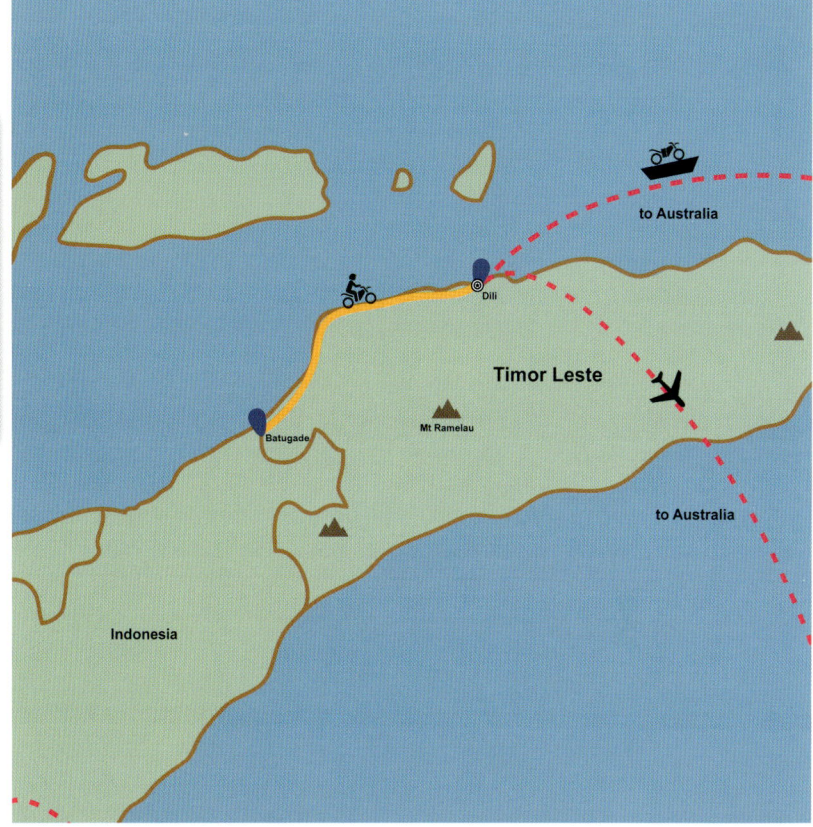

Batugade to Dili
The road to Dili was rough but the coastline was fantastic. On arrival the bike needed prepping and cleaning, ready for Australia

The roads in Timor-Leste were very poor but the coastal views eclipsed any worries about road surface, although it was obviously important to stay focused on the road. I passed some lovely deserted beaches with mangrove plants en route to Dili. On arrival in Dili I met the SDV (shipping agent) guys immediately (mid afternoon) so had time to understand what they needed: a full copy of my passport (every page? This was new ...), and to have the bike thoroughly cleaned. I had it power-hosed initially and then carried out a more detailed clean. Christmas was almost upon us, and, whilst cleaning the bike, an Australian lady from the hotel told me that, if I was on my own on Christmas Day, I could go to the orphanage with her and help out. It was a very kind offer – and it would have been nice to give something back – but it had been a long six months for me, and sometimes lonely, so I was planning to spend Christmas Day in Melbourne, Australia, with my friend, Belinda, and her family.

I completed the SDV task list and took the bike in to the shipping agent on the 17th. The first quote came in at $750 dollars (I think they were trying it on) with a final price of $520 (by removing the fairing, wing mirrors and sat nav bracket in order to lose a bit of height I got the cost down) to pack and freight the bike to Australia – apparently, cost can vary depending what else is in the container. Once I got the bike sorted I managed to book a flight for myself the next day at eight in the morning.

Batugade to Dili
Local village; local interest

THE REAL WAY ROUND

I saw loads of UN vehicles – big, white Toyota land cruisers with just a single, western-looking occupant: no car-sharing here – in Dili but only a few in remote areas, and couldn't help thinking they were in the wrong place in the city. Also noticeable were the UN staff in the handful of restaurants and bars. Riots in 2002 and 2006 suggest some representation is needed, but the degree of presence seemed unnecessary, verging on inappropriate, and I was only in Dili a couple of days.

I managed to go to a museum that evening, mostly just photographs (stunning and shocking) but these allowed me to see the extent of the problems the country experienced during its battle for independence, and the years that followed as the situation gradually stabilised. Up until 2012 a large number of Australian troops were still based here.

I wondered why I was getting some funny looks riding to Dili then realised that the 'I love Indonesia' sticker on the bike probably wasn't the best idea: according to a 2006 report, over 100,000 East Timorese died as a direct result of the Indonesian 24-year occupation.

I arrived at the airport to be met with the news that, as the last one to book on a flight that was over-subscribed, I might not get on it. Aargh! not Christmas in East Timor, please! At 7.30am I was informed that as two passengers had arrived late I could take one of their seats. I wasn't sure about this system – it didn't seem right, somehow – but I wanted to get to Australia, and an hour and ten minutes later I was in Darwin.

Dili
Dili life: markets; football – and the United Nations

Dili
In memoriam: images from Dili Museum

Australia

Dates in country	*Fri 18 Dec-Tue 26 Jan 2010*
Number of days	*39*
Population (millions)	*20*
Capital	*Canberra*
Area (km sq)	*7,687,000*
Currency	*Australian dollar*
Entry/exit points	*From Dili, Timor-Leste to Darwin, Australia. Exit from Sydney, Australia*
Total distance miles (km)/date	*21,500/ (34,600)Fri 22 Jan*
Average miles (km) per day	*70 (112) (includes a week off the bike)*
Accommodation	*80% camping/20% homes of friends and family*
Food	*The food in Asia was amazing but the relief of being able to order a full English breakfast and/or fish and chips was palpable*
Value	*Good value camping with decent facilities. Other items cost the same as the UK so not cheap – don't expect to get the budget back on track in Australia*
Rating (out of 10)	*8*

In a nutshell
Long straight roads down the middle of the country; hot and humid (particularly in the north); recognisable landmarks; familiar food; easy camping and friendly folk.

Route
Darwin to Port Augusta (south), Port Augusta to Sydney (east).

Rider notes
Great chance to get things repaired (laptop, sat nav).
Bike – Fab Yamaha service at Northern Territory Motorcycles – first tyre change at 18,000 miles (28,968km) – wow! to the Metzler Tourance tyres. The most serious bike check at Customs. Heated grips removed at Alice Springs (glue had simply perished in the humidity further north). Oil change in Sydney.
Maps – Good maps by Gregory with various titles that also detail off-road.

Australia

Aussie Aussie Aussie!
Football and Hot Rods

Rider log
Friday 18 December

I made it to Darwin airport, Australia, but this was just the first stop: I needed a flight to Melbourne.

As the bike was on the water for three days, arriving in Darwin on December 23, I couldn't collect it until the new year owing to bank holidays and opening hours of Customs/AQIS (Australian Quarantine and Inspection Service). A long-overdue service was scheduled at Northern Territory Motorcycles, just outside Darwin, planned for at least the previous two months. The work required was over and above a standard service – I wanted

After months in the Far East I was very relieved to find familiar-looking food – real classics, too!

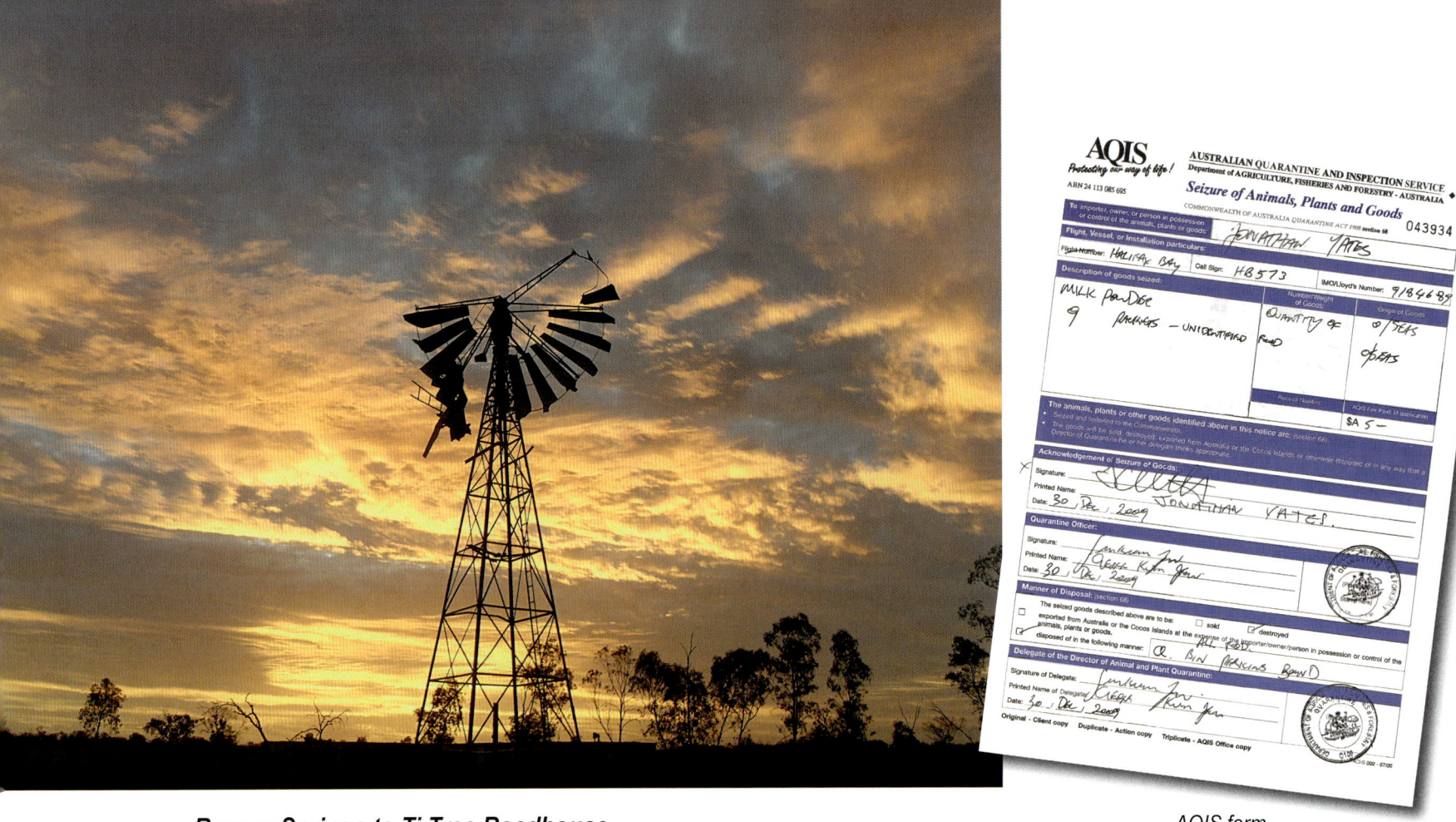

Renner Springs to Ti Tree Roadhouse
Old-style windmill water pumps can still be seen

AQIS form

Metzler Tourance tyres, for example; not a stock item as I think the Ténéré was just about to launch in Australia.

If I didn't want to spend Christmas on my own (and I didn't!), I had to get a seat on a flight to Melbourne, but all of the flights were full, and even over-subscribed. I put myself on every possible waiting list and befriended members of staff responsible for seat allocation.

Virgin Blue 6.15pm Darwin to Melbourne: 180 seats and 181 purchased tickets, and I had number 182. Online check-in enables passengers to arrive later, so it really was going to be a last-minute rush. In my favour was my limited luggage (just a day bag and helmet), as most of it was on the bike. At 5.30pm I returned to the gate to meet Gina, the ace Virgin Blue airline lady: I will always remember how helpful she was (during a year-long trip it's the unusual that stays longest in the memory), and Gina was extremely helpful. A couple of no-shows but still no confirmed seats. At 5.50pm Gina rang a customer who had not turned up and was told he was not planning to get the flight. As I was willing to pay full price I took priority over others already waiting as standby customers (who don't pay full fare). At 6.05 they put my transaction through and I was on the plane ten minutes later, which took off almost immediately. Okay, so maybe I'd queue-jumped but if you pay full price, you get the ticket ...

I'd been lucky to make these two flights: Dili-Darwin (as a reserve place/over-subscribed booking) and Darwin-Melbourne (arrive at the airport and hope I make it). I definitely couldn't have stayed in Darwin from the 18th through to when the bike arrived on the 30th: it was just too long.

I hung out in Melbourne with Belinda (who I first met in 1997 when the two of us drove from Melbourne to Perth: another great road trip) and her family, Kaz, Josh and Mia, in Fitzroy, which was pretty cool. Where they lived reminded me a lot of a fashionable London suburb – loads of cool bars – and it was great to fill up on a traditional English breakfast after Asia. Not so cool was my ear infection as I couldn't hear anything properly (tropical ear?) so I got drops, something to squirt up my nose, and some Sudafed tablets to unblock it all (pharmacies everywhere, luckily for me).

A few days before Christmas Day I was able to contact Perkins Shipping Ltd to track the bike and ring Customs and AQIS, which checks for contamination (ie seeds, mud on the bike), or if you have brought anything dodgy into the country in terms of plants or fruit, and has a reputation for being very strict. I managed to get the bike booked in with Customs/AQIS on December 30 at 10.30 in the morning for checks and admin, which would cost about AUS$200 (£137). If passed and released I could get the bike to Northern Territory Motorcycles in the afternoon for its service. Timings were tight but achievable.

A barbeque in 35°C heat in Castlemaine (two hours north of Melbourne) on Christmas Eve was a strange event for someone more used to the usual wintery conditions of England, and Christmas Day was a trip to the

Australia

local park for another barbeque under a gazebo for shade. It was a beautiful way to spend the day, which was followed by a quick game of Aussie Rules footie (more practice needed: Josh was just too quick).

The break from riding gave me chance to chat over what route I should take with various people, the general consensus being to go 'down the guts,' to enjoy the Red Centre and avoid any of the storms and possible road closures predicted for the north east, with the east coast being another option.

I left Castlemaine on December 28 (a bank holiday), dashing to the airport to make the 8.45am flight to Darwin to collect the bike. It was a great flight, and the pilot pointed out that we were flying over Lake Eyre and the Red Centre, which looked fabulous. The views really raised my anticipation levels: I was ready to get back on the bike and ride.

Free accommodation in Jingili, Darwin provided a fab base from which to get organised, set up the bike and establish my route plan. Darwin was very humid and prone to prolonged heavy downpours at this time of year, and I was reminded that it was the front end of cyclone season (the bathroom doubles up as a safe room). Safe houses and signs all around the suburbs are a reminder of the cyclone of 1974 (big and destructive!).

Wednesday 30 December

With most people still enjoying their Christmas break, this was a big day for me, and it felt a little like *The Great Escape*! By 10.30 that morning I was at Perkins Shipping to reclaim my bike from Customs/AQIS. Checking was so detailed that even a tiny dentist-style mirror was used to look under both mudguards in the search for seeds and other foreign objects. A search of my bags/tent, groundsheets and bike panniers resulted in confiscation of Chinese milk powder and cereal from Kazakhstan (understandable, really).

The officer was a nice guy and, as he had his own bike, we had some common ground about which to chat. Everyone helped move things along, and he gave me the good news that everything had passed scrutiny. With my Carnet de Passage paperwork stamped I could rebuild the bike/pack and get to the bike shop.

Completing even the smallest physical task was a sweaty job as the 80-85% humidity in Darwin was extremely difficult to cope with, and was one of the reasons why I'd decided to go straight down the middle. Even here, the temperature is usually 35 to 45 degrees, depending on actual weather.

The logistics of moving the bike around the world are interesting, time-consuming, sometimes frustrating and usually costly. At the port in Darwin they were bringing in tanks that had been over in Sumatra following the earthquake. The teams sorting the freight were busy and I needed to jump the queue. The guys wanted a 'slab' of beers to allow this but I was at my limit in terms of spending following the flight saga and freighting of the bike.

Northern Territory Motorcycles was about 10km (6 miles) south east of the port, and we had been in touch over the internet from Indonesia and on the phone from Melbourne to give the shop chance to order any parts needed for the service.

Once again I received amazing customer service as Northern Territory Motorcycles was incredibly helpful. I dropped the bike at 2pm on December 30 and had it back the next day (New Year's Eve) at 2.30 that afternoon, which meant I could resume riding on January 1, 2010. A top job from the 'top enders,' as they're called in Darwin. Everything on the bike was just fab with the exception of the sat nav which refused to charge. I really needed to get

Darwin
A detailed search by customs and AQIS in the extreme humidity of Darwin was draining, but, following its service the Ténéré looked and rode amazingly – was I developing feelings for this machine?

this fixed before reaching South America, although I did manage to download a map for the majority of Argentina/Chile whilst in Darwin.

New Year's Eve was a small affair with a few fireworks at the marina: my thoughts were concenrated on riding the next day ...

Friday January 1, 2010 – on the road again

My tour through Australia can be split into two parts: south, and straight down the middle on the Stuart Highway; east from Port Augusta to Sydney.

Exiting Darwin on the Stuart Highway (also known as Explorer Highway), I rode south to Katherine. After its $1200 (£800) service the bike

Katherine to Renner Springs
Size matters – road train and truck stops. Love the stickers on the back bar: 'Prices subject to change, according to customer's attitude'!

was in good shape, running as smoothly as the day I left the UK some 18,000 miles ago.

It was very humid in Katherine, which resulted in a terrible night's sleep – even moving outside the tent didn't help – and knowing there were crocs about made me a tad nervous, anyway. A worthwhile trek and swim in the stunning Katherine Gorge meant a second night camping at the friendly Springvale Homestead (so friendly the owners let me have the second night for free – after eighteen days in Australia, I'd spent just $10 (£7) on accommodation).

Further south the next stop was Mataranka to refuel the bike with unleaded, and myself with a couple of the town's famous and delicious steak-stuffed pies – good eating whilst reading about one of the Northern Territories' obsessions: big rigs or road trains. Sometimes comprising five trailers, 2.5km (1.5 miles) are required to overtake a road train at full speed – so choose your moment, as it's undoubtedly pretty scary to get stuck overtaking one of those with traffic coming in the opposite direction.

Common sights along the monotonously long, straight roads were bright red termite mounds sticking sharply out of the ground; road trains; road kill, and bits of old tyres which have sheared off cars and trucks. The occasional break at historical hostelries such as the Daly Waters Pub provided refreshment and some different points of interest, like the bric-a-brac type collection of automotive memorabilia which was almost a roadside museum.

By Renner Springs I noticed that, despite the cloud cover, my face had burnt bright red. The continual wet weather and long distances were becoming heavy-going so it was good news to learn – according to locals – that dry weather was about two days' ride away. Just south of Tennant Creek the weather did improve, and I was able to shed the waterproofs and have a walkabout to stretch my legs at Devils Marbles, circular-shaped stones balanced on top of each other which look like they have simply been dropped into the desert.

I was stopped and breathalysed by the police just outside of Tennant Creek. The policeman was from Bradford in England, and had spotted the Colin Appleyard sticker on the bike. (Appleyard is a well-respected Yorkshire bike dealer which helped prep the bike, as well as throwing in a few freebies in exchange for having its sticker on the bike: not quite Moto GP sponsorship but it all helps ...) I'm pretty sure that the breath test was an excuse to stop me for a chat! His advice was not to stay in the next village, as there was a 'community' there (I think he meant aboriginal community), which 'might turn the bike over.' I don't know, but it seemed a statement with racist undertones, I had picked up on similar conversations in Darwin: unfortunately, some non-indigenous Australians still regard the aboriginal population with a degree of prejudice.

An overnight stop at the Ti Tree Road House – 8 dollars (£5) to camp round the back and use the facilities – led to a night of unexpected jukebox jollity with archetypal Australian songs as *Ringer from the Top End* and the all-time classic *Down Under* by Men at Work – WOW!

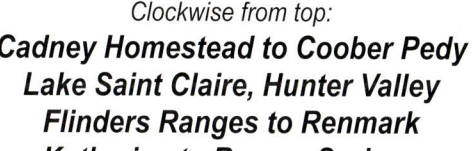

Clockwise from top:
Cadney Homestead to Coober Pedy
Lake Saint Claire, Hunter Valley
Flinders Ranges to Renmark
Katherine to Renner Springs

*Roadside views varied ...
but landscapes are BIG in Oz*

THE REAL WAY ROUND

Flinders Ranges to Renmark *(left)*

Mildura to West Wyalong *(above)*
Australia has great camping facilities. Note the Coleman petrol stove (ideal as you don't need to carry additional fuel; just drain it from the tank), and the Leatherman Wave multitool, which can 'get you out of jail' in many situations

By January 5 I had made it through the Tropic of Capricorn and arrived at Alice Springs (18,284 miles/29,425km) where a local bike dealer helped me replace my heated grips with standard ATV items, as the humidity of Indonesia and Darwin had caused the throttle grip to slip on the handlebar, making holding a steady speed impossible. It seems they weren't very well fitted by SMC in Sheffield as there was tape between the grip and the handlebar, which means they weren't a perfect fit anyway.

Alice Springs is a great base from which to explore a number of gorges and maybe do a little off-road riding on the Larapinta Trail which cuts back to Ayres Rock. However, the wet weather and forecast of more rain meant that staying on the tarmac was the sensible option: ironically, in the middle of the Red Centre I experienced the wettest weather since leaving England.

I rode the gorges with a Japanese rider (Kazuya) who had hired a bike for a two-week holiday. He rode with a big smile on his face that I could see in his mirrors. He was loving every minute, which was refreshing to see and a reminder of how lucky I was to be making this global trip.

The rain was so heavy there was talk of Alice Springs flooding as the River Todd could burst its banks, so it was a race to get my kit dry and get out before the weather got too bad to leave Alice Springs. The open desert and weather front made for challenging crosswinds, equal to the gusts in Kazakhstan, during the ride to Ayers Rock, Uluru. Arriving at such world-famous landmarks really brought home how far I had ridden although still only halfway round at 18,816 miles (12,935km). The National Park guide was beaming when she told me that only 3% of visitors get to see the rock with waterfalls, but as it kept raining I was in that lucky 3%, and the rock looked fantastic.

Next morning rumours were circulating that a number of roads had been cut off due to the heavy rain, but I decided to push on anyway and head toward Kings Canyon. Based on previous experience rumours are often exaggerated and 'impassable' is usually quite passable. However, on this occasion the rumours weren't exaggerated and the road to the National Park area was impassable, covered by almost two metres (six feet) of water. Three cars had already tried and become stuck. It was 2.30pm so the only choice was to stay at Kings Creek Station and ride back to the canyon the next day if the road was clear. Luckily for me, this all fell into place and I got to Kings Canyon National Park, which was very impressive.

On the journey south, despite overcast skies everything looked vibrant as the rainfall had given rise to some lovely deep green and red colours that looked fantastic. I just hoped the roads stayed clear: my main concern was getting stuck somewhere because all of the floodways (channels for diverting flood water) kept giving way and blocking the road. A local who advised me not to go off-road said the Red Centre 'turns to porridge' when wet, and he was right as it was soft, boggy, and unrideable for any distance. I was glad I took his advice in preference to that of the lady at the National Park with all her weather radars and satellite pictures, as she told me it was fine! At the

Ayres Rock (Uluru) *(above)*

Devils Marbles *(left)*

Flinders Ranges *(overleaf)*

Recognisable landmarks increased my sense of achievement at having ridden halfway round the world. Only the same again to get home ...

THE REAL WAY ROUND

end of the day, when it comes to making a decision, it's down to you to judge who has the most realistic view and whose advice you trust.

On leaving Kings Canyon the next morning I saw wild horses for the first time, milling around at the edge of the road, drinking from pools of water that had appeared following the latest downpour. The horses – shiny and wet – pranced about, luxuriating, I imagine, in the rain and having access to fresh drinking water.

The rain affected everything: lizards sunbathed in the middle of the road, trying to dry out; cattle and kangaroos drank from pools at the roadside; road trains kicked up spray as they hurtled past; cattle grids became slippery and treacherous, and birds of prey gorged themselves on the increased road kill, though sometimes ending up as part of this if hit by the road trains that thundered by.

Finally, just before Cadney Roadhouse (Sunday 10 January), the clouds dispersed and the sky turned blue: it felt like I was in the desert. The weather had been so extreme that the Ghan Train (named after the Afghan cameleers who once traversed this route, this train will take you from one edge of Australia to the other, through its very centre) had to be turned back as the tracks had been washed away – a first, apparently.

Coober Pedy ('white man underground') was an interesting opal

Ayres Rock (Uluru) to Watarrka National Park
Heavy rains cut off a number of roads and made off-roading the Red Centre a no-no

Cadney Homestead to Coober Pedy (above)

Lake Saint Claire, Hunter Valley (right)
Easy riding, and well set up for bikers (as you'd expect)

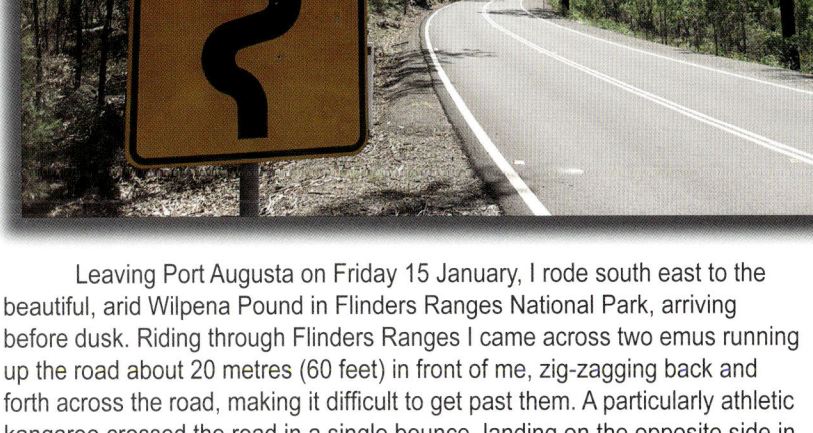

mining town which still had a number of functioning mines. Conical mounds of earth line the road as you enter the town, giving the impression of a lunar landscape combined with the wild west. With over 250,000 mine shafts created by independent opal prospectors, there appeared to be unlimited amounts of dynamite about, so I wasn't surprised to hear that, during a local dispute, an angry miner had attempted to blow up the police station.

My arrival at Port Augusta (home to my cousin, Wez, and his young family) took the mileage to 19,996 (32,180km). This was a great place to simply hang out, recover after the ride south, and go fishing in my cousin's boat, barbequeing crabs in the evening – totally Australian, mate! It also gave me a chance to plan the next stages of the trip, booking a Qantas flight from Sydney to Buenos Aires on 27 January, which could also freight the bike. I had to be in Sydney a week prior to organise freighting of the bike.

The bike was running smoothly still but my technical gadgets were not faring as well. The laptop was knackered and the sat nav charger had completely given up the ghost. Luckily, Garmin has its head office in Sydney, and after explaining what it was I was trying to do, we arranged to meet on January 20 when I was in Sydney to see what could be done. Other replacements required included my 'sunnies,' (sunglasses: constantly breaking pairs of these), 12 volt charger and tent pegs; the camera was on the blink but just about hanging in there.

Leaving Port Augusta on Friday 15 January, I rode south east to the beautiful, arid Wilpena Pound in Flinders Ranges National Park, arriving before dusk. Riding through Flinders Ranges I came across two emus running up the road about 20 metres (60 feet) in front of me, zig-zagging back and forth across the road, making it difficult to get past them. A particularly athletic kangaroo crossed the road in a single bounce, landing on the opposite side in the scrub. He was so quick – and deadly to hit on a bike.

I camped overnight at Wilpena Pound, and was woken the next morning by a Wallaby trying to eat my food, and tugging at some of the bags

THE REAL WAY ROUND

Ti Tree Roadhouse, Alice Springs
Road signs are there for a reason: ignore them at your peril ...

Flinders Ranges to Renmark
There are strict quarantine rules and fines regarding moving fruit and veg across states, so keep receipts to prove where fruit was bought, and chuck the banned products

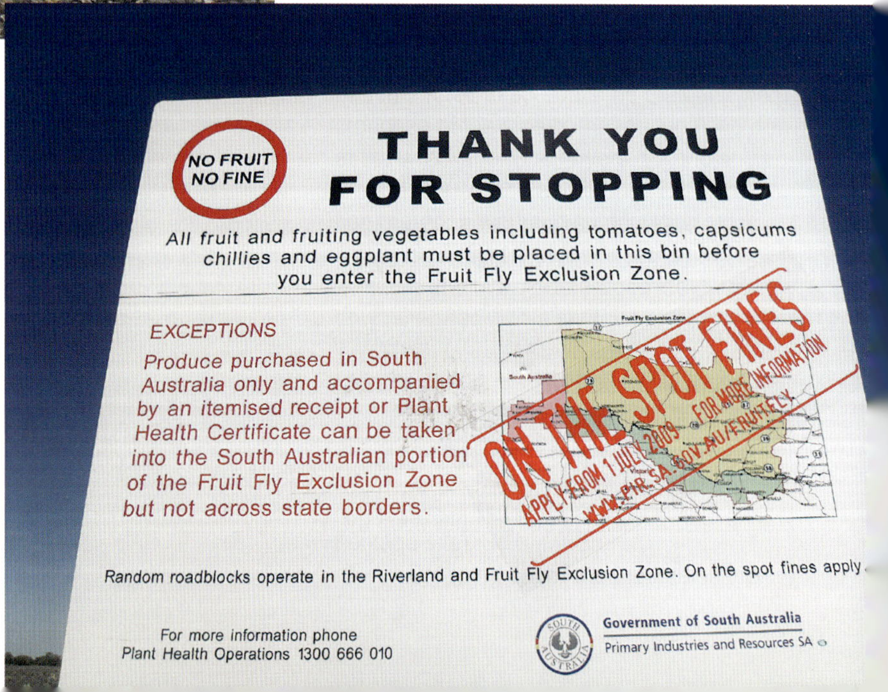

on my bike. I couldn't get rid of the little fella, he was pulling on the luggage strapping on my bike and hopping all over the place. Finally, I tried standing on his tail in an effort to get him to leave, and he didn't half run!

From Flinders Ranges I headed east, picking up the Murray River which runs through a serious fruit growing area with vineyards and fruit farms of apples, oranges, melons ... every fruit you can think of. When crossing states, all fruit has to be disposed of at certain border points to avoid the spread of fruit flies (which destroy crops), and there are heavy fines for those caught flouting the rules.

Continuing to ride further east, away from the river, the landscape – a combination of farming and scrubland – was baked dry, with dust tornados on the horizon and really strong crosswinds. A few oversized trucks came my way –– a good reason to concentrate on the road. The red haze created by a sand storm travelling across the road is unnerving: it looks impressive but I wouldn't want to be caught in one – scary riding.

Australia

Approaching Sydney I stopped on the eastern side of the Blue Mountains to plan my ride to Garmin HQ the following morning, and then on to the airport in the afternoon. The ride through the Blue Mountains with wooded valleys and many cliffs was lovely.

It was ironic having to stop and ask for directions to Garmin HQ (on the edge of Parramatta, a suburb of Sydney) the next morning, but Garmin didn't disappoint, and I was soon equipped with a new charger. Great service and a huge relief that I had this before South America.

Then it was on to acquire a Dangerous Goods Certificate (AUS$100/£65) from Dangerous Goods Management (DGM) so that I could freight the bike the following week. Next came a meeting at DPEX, Qantas' freight agency. My bike was booked on the same flight as me (well, if they could fit it on – it all felt a little hit-and-miss, despite the AUS$4000/£2600) freight fee to Buenos Aires.

Other than having to stump up this rather large fee, it was a successful day with everything completed by 2.30 that afternoon, which left time to find a campsite close to Sydney. Rockdale was 10km (6 miles) from the airport, a 15-minute walk from the beach, had good facilities and was close to the city: perfect! I still had the bike until the 25th of the month so left Rockdale and headed north to Lake Saint Clair for a few days, riding through Wollemi and Yengo National Park, cutting through Hunter Valley on Route 69, a famous biker route. It was good to see lots of bikers on the road for the first time in ages, even though the riding approach is very different on a 2-3 hour jaunt after work compared to that of someone on a global tour, and I think I held up a few on the twisty sections. The temperature was exhausting – the hottest day in Sydney in five years – 43°C and 39° around the lake.

I was back in Sydney by Sunday 24 January with a total mileage of 21,812 (35,103km) after riding halfway round the world. Dropping off the bike at the freight agent on Monday 25 January, there was a little more paperwork to do, then I disconnected the battery (fuel was already on reserve as I'd cruised the city the night before); repacked the bike and my clothes; attended to some Customs formalities, and returned to the city, where I had a couple of drinks and relaxed before my flight to Buenos Aires in a couple of days.

Visit Veloce on the web – www.veloce.co.uk/www.velocebooks.com
Details of all books in print • Special offers • New book news • Gift vouchers • Forum

Argentina
(including forays into Chile, Antarctica and Bolivia)

Dates in country	Wed 27 Jan-Mon 22 Feb (Antarctica); Sat 6 Mar-Wed 7 April
Number of days	Argentina 45 days, my route taking me briefly into Chile 4 days; Antarctica 13 days, and Bolivia 2 days
Population (millions)	51
Capital	Buenos Aires – best city of the trip: outstanding food; wine; culture, and excellent value
Area (km sq)	2,767,000
Currency	Peso
Entry/exit points	From Sydney, Australia, flying Qantas to Buenos Aires. Exit into Chile (various occasions) at Punta Delgada (south); El Turbio (south); Paso de Jama (north)
Total distance miles (km)/date	26,686 (42,947)/Fri 26 Mar
Average miles (km) per day	250-300 (402-482) (excludes days in Antarctica)
Accommodation	90% camping with a few hostels in the Tierra del Fuego Province
Food	Empanadas (bit like a pasty but better – great road food); parrilla (steak BBQ: Argentinian steak on a grill cannot be beaten; suggest combine with a Malbec from Salta). Mate tea. Andes beer
Value	Incredible quality and value
Rating (out of 10)	10

In a nutshell

If only I'd had more time ... Argentina is huge, but it's easy to underestimate this and the diversity of what it has to offer: lakes; coastline; mountains; a Red Centre that knocks Australia's into a cocked hat, and even glaciers – it really does have everything. I won't comment here about the quality of the steak and wine, except to say that both are some of the best in the world due to the country's ideal conditions for wine-growing and beef farming, and a winning combination for any biker in need of refuelling!

Route

South – Buenos Aires, Tandil, south down the Atlantic coast Ruta 3, Pedro

Argentina

Buenos Aires
It was always a relief to see the bike after freighting it from one country to another, for obvious reasons. Argentina is football-crazy: Asociación del Fútbol Argentino

What's on the menu?
The standard of food and drink was amazing, and parrilla (grilled meat), empanada (stuffed bread or pastry baked or fried), and mate tea (traditional South American infused drink) are three of the best offerings

Lodo, Penisula Valdes, Puerto Madryn, Rada Tilly (Comodoro Rivadavia), Puerto San Julián, Rio Gallegos, Rio Grande, Ushuaia (trip to Antarctica). North – Ushuaia, Rio Grande, Puerto Natales, Puerto Montt, San Carlos de Bariloche, from Zapala (landscapes turned arid and desert – Argentina is vast), General Alvear, Lújan De Cuyo, San Juan, San Agustin de Valle Fertil, Belén, Tafí del Valle, Salta.

THE REAL WAY ROUND

Rider notes

Municipal campsites are excellent – great setup for camping.
Bike – Incredibly strong winds (100km/60mph). Ripio (unsealed road) required a steady approach, so a 'performance ride' not possible here as it's necessary to focus on making it to your destination: exhausting riding, in some instances. You won't beat Nick Sanders' record-breaking 32-day world circumnavigation, but why would you want to when there's so much to see and experience? Salta is a good base for a final bike service (has a Yamaha dealer) before heading further north.
Maps – Producciones Carto Graficas/tourist road map; available for most South American countries.

Rider log

Touched down in Buenos Aires – the bike on the same Qantas flight – on Wednesday 27 January. The time difference means the bike and I left Sydney at 11am in the morning to arrive at Buenos Aires at 10am the same morning, well but shattered.

It's never simple recovering the bike from an airport –
- Finding the right office was a nightmare
- Office roulette: directed to three or four with little result
- Serious language barrier – did anyone speak English?
- Paid taxes of 1275 peso/£165

Buenos Aires
City art and demonstrations. The streets of Buenos Aires were a giant easel for those with artistic talent – and a message for the world. Stand aside, Banksy ...

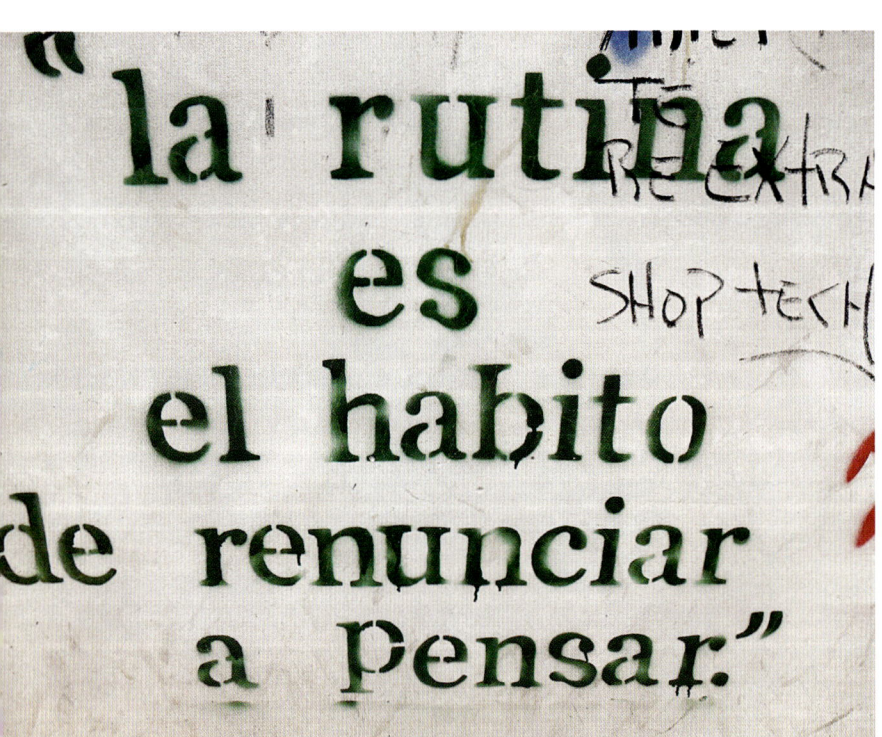

(Routine is the habit of giving up thinking)

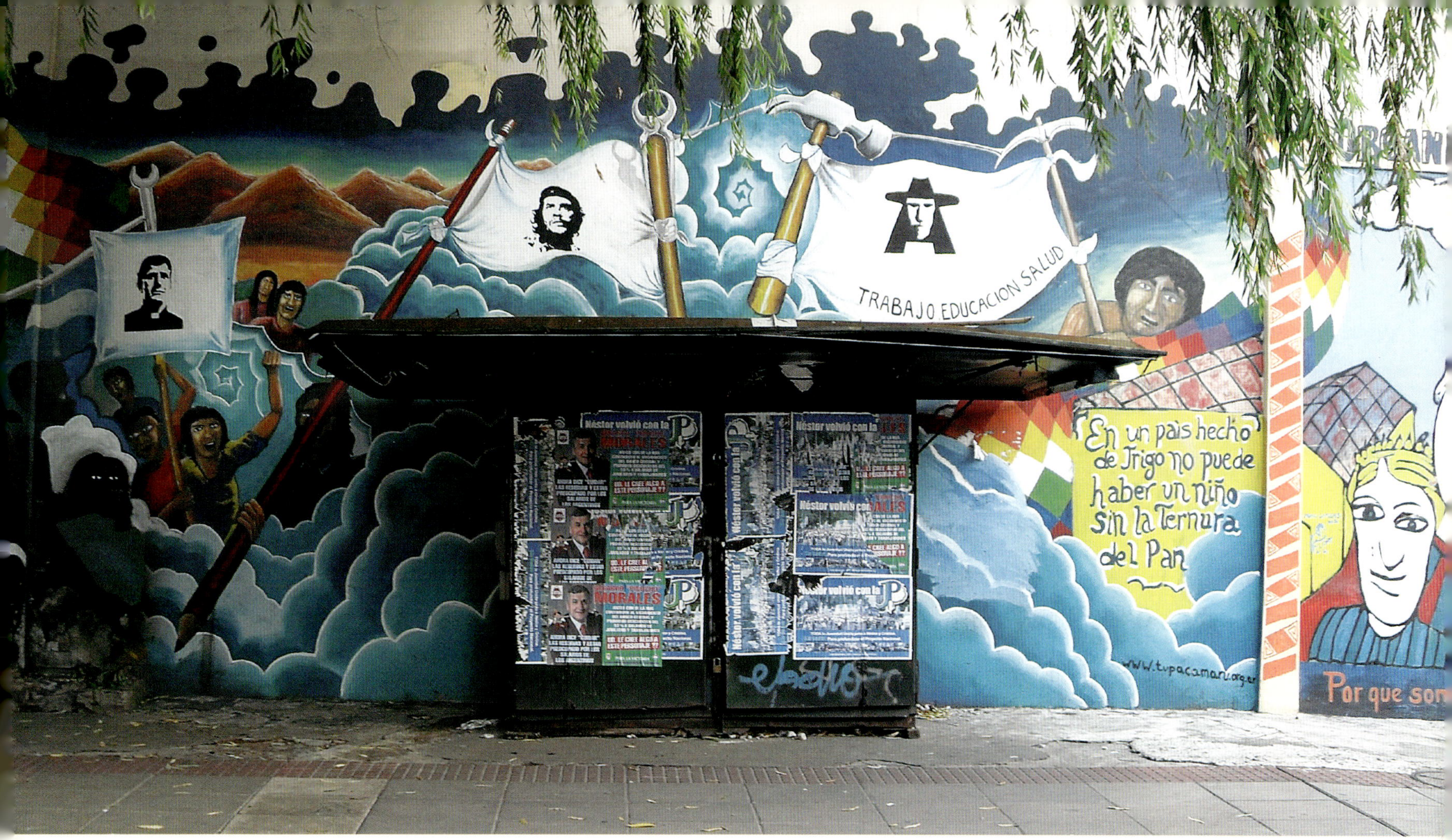
TRABAJO EDUCACION SALUD
En un pais hecho de Trigo no puede haber un niño sin la Ternura del Pan
www.tupacamaru.org.ar

TETRA

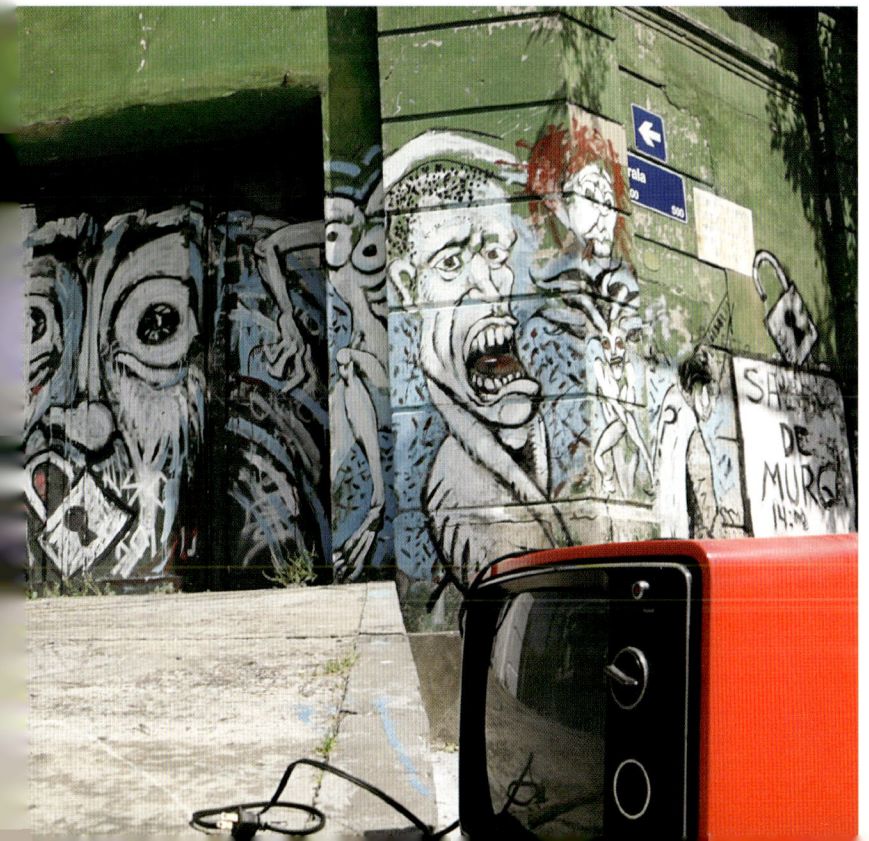

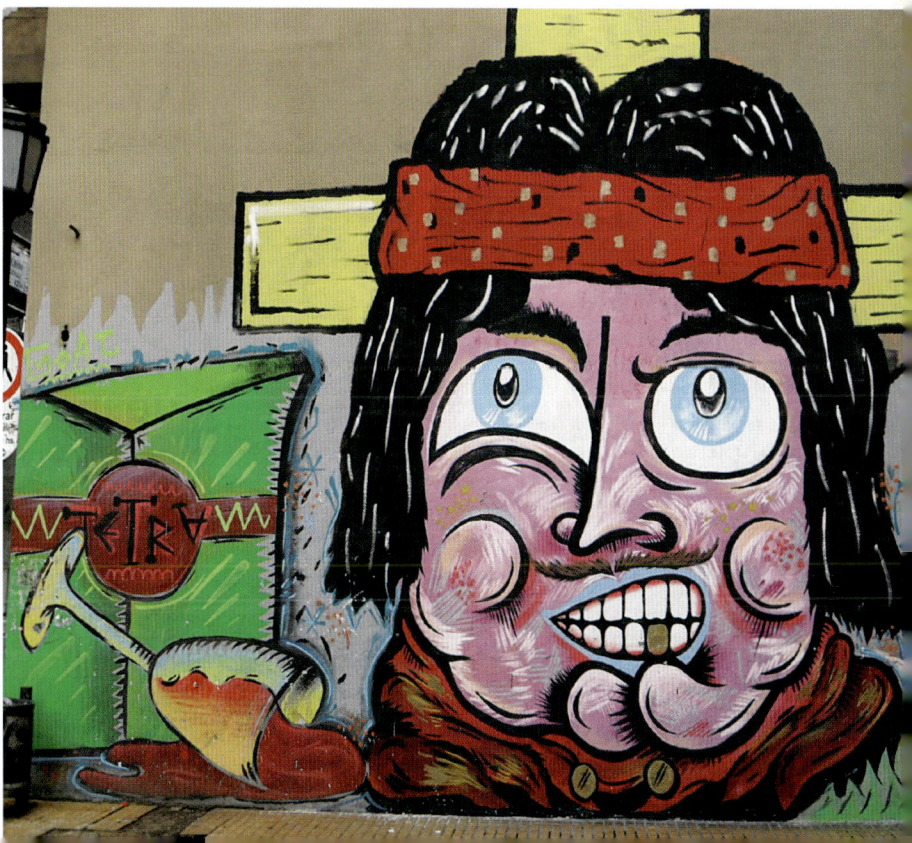

- 35°C and shattered from the flight; walking between terminals and the freight area was hard work in such heat
- Discovered bike insurance required to enable release
- Given the address of insurance office in the city
- Bus into city centre to try and organise insurance
- Arrive at 4pm – ATM insurance open until 6pm
- Two floors of motorbike riders also getting insurance
- Insurance packages for Argentina, Chile and Peru available
- Get necessary paperwork to return to airport the next day and release the bike
- Find budget hotel in lovely district of San Telmo, Buenos Aires

    The overall vibrancy, combined with superb value for money, make Buenos Aires a brilliant city – and colourful, thanks to graffiti artists who, overnight, leave their interesting

Buenos Aires
It's impossible to escape the fact that Argentinians are passionate about football

social commentary. Throw in a few Spanish lessons for essential basics (unleaded petrol = gasoline sin plomo), recuperation, and bulking up at the parillas (steak barbeques), and the time flew by. A football match at Club Atlético River Plate and a trip to La Boca area showed the Argentinians are seriously passionate about football, and, ultimately, the crowd was more entertaining than the sloppy football. Nightly, I was reminded of the poverty here as the cartoneros (named after cartón, the Spanish word for cardboard) walk from the shantytowns and poor districts of the city on the edge of town, towards the centre and wealthy neighborhoods to look for valuables or recyclable material in the rubbish bags left on every street corner. Each family had its own pitch, and I would see the same mother and her teenage daughters on the corner of Humberto Primo, San Telmo (where I lodged). They turned up for work, collected up the bin bags, put them in a big pile in the corner, and went through every inch of rubbish, pulling out anything that was of value or recyclable, and then rebagging the rubbish. I was sad to see this in amongst the emerging wealth of Buenos Aires but, when markets crashed in 2001, the numbers of cartoneros swelled as thousands of newly unemployed workers lost their stable lives and joined the ranks.

The day I left the car park where I was storing my bike, security staff and resident police officers wished me good luck, and one officer kissed me on both cheeks – customary in Argentina – though the others noted my

Buenos Aires
The infamous La Boca area; home of Diego Maradona. Tevez also played at Boca Juniors

Argentina

Tandil to Pedro Luro   **Las Grutas to Puerto Pirámides**

Long ride south on roads toll-free for bikes, complete with great camps; lots of other road trippers (5-star luxury of a Mercedes bus); sunflower oil, and oil drilling

Rada Tilly to Puerto San Julian

THE REAL WAY ROUND

surprise and uncomfortable body language. The single embrace became a group hug, as laughing and joking, everyone joined in: quite a contrast to the Ukrainian police back in August.

Highway toll booths charged just half a peso (around 6 pence), so next to nothing, really, and hardly worth the effort by the time I'd stopped, taken off my gloves, messed about getting the change, and tried to understand how much was due from the guy in the toll booth, whilst cars behind honked impatiently and people shouted at me to get out of the city. The second of two tolls I passed through was a real trial as I couldn't get my glove off to find my change!

I finally arrived at a place called Tandil and set up camp for the night, the 180 mile (289km) ride there taking total mileage to 22,038 (35,466km) on Saturday 6 February. I met a lovely couple; the lady (Carrina) spoke really good English and was actually an English teacher, and the guy (Pekitas) was a mini bus driver. There are quite a few people in Argentina making roadtrips,

Esperanza to El Calafate
Tough conditions: note the sign

Rio Grande to Ushuaia
Tierra Del Fuego was stunning; the weather there in stark contrast to the north

El Calafate
Landmarks in Patagonia: Perito Moreno Glacier, which covers a bigger surface area than Buenos Aires; the extremes of Torres del Paine (and overleaf)

so there's always someone to chat to and plan routes with in the evenings at campsites. A constant feature of the Atlantic coast is the cold, strong wind that increases in intensity the further south you venture, making the ride difficult and tiring in places. Struggling to gain momentum in Argentina, I just couldn't seem to hit the same sweet spot I'd had in Indonesia, and wondered if the weather was part of the reason for this.

Ruta 3 on the east coast is not the most exciting of roads, but one highlight en route south was Peninsula Valdes, home to elephant seals, penguins, llamas, armadillos, loads of little creatures, big creatures, all kinds of stuff, snakes, etc. Didn't see any whales, though (wrong time of year apparently – try January).

Some really difficult and tough crosswinds encountered heading south, including a few sandstorms (much bigger and stronger than in Australia). Apart from the wind, general temperatures were quite extreme: baking hot (33-35°C) in the daytime and so cold at night that it was not unusual to sleep with a fleece on.

Argentina

Rio Grande to Esperanza
(left)

Esperanza to El Calafate
(above)
The geography of Chile and Argentina generates plenty of border crossings. Good riding in remote parts of Chile, and a chance to compare notes with other bikers

Puerto Montt to Villa La Angostra
(right)

By Rio Grande the weather had got the better of me and I opted for a backpacker-type lodge in preference to camping: only a few pesos more, and I was able to dry the kit. Though now constantly cold and often wet, the scenery had started to improve on the approach to the Chilean border, the crossing of which took a couple of hours. One hundred miles of Chilean ripio (rubble!) later, I crossed back into Argentina at San Sebastián and then on to the amazing Tierra Del Fuego (Land of Fire), an archipelago off the southernmost tip of the South American mainland, across the Strait of Magellan.

The next day (19 February) brought a real landmark: 144 miles (231km) to Ushuaia, the most southern city in the world, and total mileage to get there 24,228 (38,991km). It was a short day's riding, which was good because the snow-capped mountains, rivers, huge swathes of wilderness, and alpine forests were just stupendous, plus there were lots of amazing National Parks and places worth seeing in Patagonia, such as Tierra del Fuego National Park, Francisco P Moreno National Park, Seven Lakes Road (Bariloche), and Peninsula Valdes.

The next couple of days were spent relaxing and seeing National Parks, glaciers, lakes, and deep green forests and wildlife in one of the most stunning parts of the world. Around Ushuaia marina the number of yachts flying European flags were many, and I imagined that this might be my next adventure: to sail around the world. I'd had this location marked as the most southern point of my journey, until, that is, I decided to take advantage of a last-minute Antarctic expedition leaving on 23 Feb: too great an opportunity to miss, and it would give me time off the bike after the ride south.

Antarctica: Tuesday 23 February-Sunday 7 March

The Antarctic is the most remote place on the planet, with the highest mountains and incredible marine wildlife.

Our ship, the Akademik Ioffe, was built as a spy/scientific research vessel, and was captained by a Canadian expedition team and run by a Russian crew. Icebergs, whales, seals, albatross, penguins, loads of different birds and mountains were plentiful, as well as simply stunning scenery in the Beagle Channel, a calm passage of water that leads to the more ferocious Drake Passage, where three oceans meet and fight for a route through the gap between Ushuaia and Antartica. On both outward and return journeys we experienced very rough conditions which were definitely not for the faint-

cnt'd page 137

Antarctica
The most southerly continent, and worth a visit if you get to Ushuaia and have the time. On average, it is the coldest, driest, windiest, and most mountainous continent: just a shame I couldn't take the bike (and overleaf)

THE REAL WAY ROUND

Argentina

Valle Union to Belén
UK roadside signs bearing warnings such as '140 casualties in the last five years – Ride Safe' have much less impact than the roadside memorials in Argentina. It's not known what significance the plastic bottles have but they are usual

Villa La Angostra to Zapala
(far left)

hearted. Despite this, it was one of the best experiences of the trip, which, ironically, did not involve riding! The two weeks' full board on the ship was a much-needed holiday within the trip, and an awesome experience: highly recommended; the pictures say it all.

Pushing north: 8 March/24,300 miles/39,107km
Whilst in Antarctica an earthquake measuring 8 on the Richter Scale shook Chilean towns and cities, including the capital, Santiago. The epicentre was Concepción.

My original plan was to ride north through Chile, but earthquake damage was so severe (roads and buildings had been completely destroyed), and fuel hard to find that I had to come up with an alternative route. My last day in Ushuaia had been spent catching up on the news and changing the bike's oil, and I was ready to move on. It was nice to see the sat nav compass point north as it meant I was on the home straight, with about 15,000 miles (24,140km) to ride.

The first part of the route was familiar. Through Rio Grande the winds welcomed me back (gusts of 100km/60mph had been forecast), both difficult and probably dangerous but best to ignore that. There's no other way out of Patagonia so I had to grin and bear it, and put the stories about motorcyclists being gusted off their machines to the back of my mind. I returned to the café next to the budget backpacker hostel to fill up on steak and chips, with a couple eggs whacked on top, for less than a fiver, including a drink – was this a Wetherspoon Steak Club, I wondered?

The weather was rough, and worse was forecast. I decided to take the ferry on the east coast of Chile, leaving Puerto Natales for Puerto Montt, Chile, which would give me chance to check out Perito Moreno Glacier and Torres Del Paine National Park en route to Natales, and avoid the draining weather and conditions further north. I still had some distance to cover over the next four months, which was important to keep in mind as tiredness and riding long distances aren't a good mix. The ferry was there for a reason, too: yes, backpackers were on it but also a heap of freight and local cars – road conditions in this part of the world are notorious at this time of year.

Most of the riding in Southern Patagonia is done leaning into the wind at an acute angle – the gusts so strong they would get under my helmet and lift it if not for the chin strap holding it in place. On the ripio I could feel the bike moving/sliding sideways in the wind. I ended up stranded in Esperanza (Santa Cruz Province) in the middle of nowhere due to the winds – a safe haven rather than a destination – but only for one night. For anyone planning a similar trip do not underestimate the weather conditions in Southern Patagonia – time it carefully and build in a few extra days; it's very exposed everywhere with little shelter, should this be needed in an emergency, say, and it can be hours before help may arrive. I adjusted my speed according to weather and road conditions, and watched the sat nav count down the miles. On the approach to El Calafate things calmed down; the road got a bit twisty and a great view over a lake came into view – fabulous.

At the border crossing from Argentina to Chile (at Rio Turbio), the officer wanted to go through my bags and panniers first. He was looking for food, really (they don't look for drugs as such, though I'm sure it would not have been pleasant if he had found some ...) but are obsessed about food crossing borders. Honey is always asked about but I couldn't decide whether this was because the guards wanted some or it was high on their contraband list.

I had a day at the stunning Torres del Paine National Park before taking the bike to Navimag Ferries the next day (Monday 15 March; total mileage 25,130 (40,442km). About a hundred people were onboard, plus horses, cows and other freight, plus a trailer containing six KTM bikes. En route we docked at a very small fishing village island called Eden, and dropped off a few passengers and supplies. On Friday 19 March we docked at Puerto Montt – I honked at a few shipmates as I left and rode north to Bariloche's seven lakes. The change in climate was both dramatic and a relief, and I was soon back in the groove.

Sunday 21 March was one of the biggest days of the trip, riding 448 miles (720km) from Zapala to General Alvear (a midway point in Argentina; I camped in the middle of a vineyard). For the first time in months I had the

THE REAL WAY ROUND

Eden
*Island life in Chile. When I got back to the UK and re-insured my bike, the guy at the call centre asked "Is your bike garaged?"
I pictured the rickety sheds on Eden – which are typical of most 'garages' I came across – and chuckled*

Argentina

San Miguel de Tucuman to Salta
Gigantic cacti: head-to-head with a llama

Puerto Montt to Villa La Angostra
(and opposite, bottom) Roadside treats: it doesn't come any fresher than this

wind at my back; relaxed and 'woo-hooing' into my helmet. Riding north under warm sun and blue skies I had the Andes to my left and vineyards to my right – it was perfect. The further north I rode the longer the siesta period, it seemed (they must be temperature-related). In any South/Latin American town everything closed between 1 and 7pm, which meant I couldn't get a single thing as nowhere was open. If I arrived somewhere during this time, I usually decided I might just as well carry on riding ...

By San Agustin de Valle Fertil the landscape had changed to desert scenes: cacti; eagles thermalling above me; horses and goats at the roadside, and vast remote landscapes complete with warm winds. Very different to places such as Indonesia where a village popped up every half hour, I could ride for hours in Argentina without seeing anybody or anything (in fact, I'd started carrying extra water (5 litres on the back of the bike) for this very reason.

I arrived at Ischigualasto Provincial Park, home of the extraordinary Valle de la Luna (Valley of the Moon, with its almost moon-like surface), and Talampaya National Park, a UNESCO World Heritage site since 2000 that features huge canyons. In all these National Parks there's a great history of finding dinosaur skeletons, and you can imagine these massive creatures roaming there as the landscape is hugely Jurassic with valleys of rocks. The ride north took me through desert, and small, isolated villages and towns, usually located in lush river valleys. I saw shepherds and cowboys; rode mountainous routes through the clouds, over red cliffs and into canyons.

cnt'd page 142

Valle Union to Belén

The riding in the Red Centre of Argentina was incredible, and the small towns there gave rise to some funny moments. Do you think this pub has WiFi? And could this be the smallest petrol station in the world?

San Miguel de Tucuman to Salta (above)

Desert homes

Mendoza to San Juan (below)

THE REAL WAY ROUND

In the northern town of Salta (my final destination in Argentina) I was due to meet Diego, a guy I'd met in Antarctica, and service the bike, before continuing north and on into Central America. Salta is great: a very welcoming city that's a decent size, with fab bars – and a Yamaha dealership! In true Argentinian style, the completion date of the service was Wednesday 7 April, which meant I had some time to kill, so headed north into Bolivia with Diego's brother and friends in their 4x4, taking in Salar de Uyuni, Potosi, Laguna Colorada, and El Tatio, encircled by volcanoes and more than 80 gurgling geysers, high in the Andes.

By Thursday 8 April I was riding again, and heading for the Chilean border to pass through into Peru. I was riding just above 4000 metres (13,000 feet) with spectacular scenery all about me, though could feel that the bike had lost performance due to this altitude. The service (new tyres – Michelin Anakee – oil, filter and brake pads) did the job, though.

San Agustin to Valle Union
Riding on the moon — Argentina's central desert is home to Valle de la Luna and National Park Talampaya: don't miss these

San Juan to San Agustin (right)

Belén to San Miguel de Tucuman (above)

La Quiaca to Uyuni, Bolivia (top)
The villages across South America seemed basic but were always friendly – and it was always possible to get what I needed

THE REAL WAY ROUND

Valle Union to Belén
Larking about with cowboys who were having a few drinks after a heavy shift in the heat

Salta
I got an unexpected ride in a police car when my bike was towed away due to a parking infringement (never park on a taxi rank). The police were very helpful and released the bike the same afternoon, once a few fines had been paid. Apparently, it can take three days to complete this process so a financial sweetener was called for to expedite this

Uyuni to Laguna Colorado, Bolivia
Pack your shades; the glare is unbelievable on the world's biggest salt plain

La Quiaca to Uyuni, Bolivia
Refreshments

THE REAL WAY ROUND

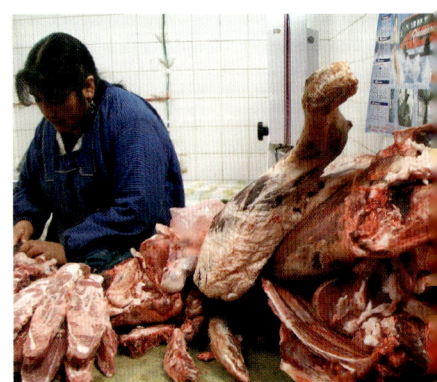

Uyuni, Bolivia
*Market-day,
Bolivian-style*

Salta to Paso de Jama (and overleaf)
The last few days riding north to Chile to exit Argentina for the final time were fantastic, as I discovered one of the best sections of road in the world; had a little unscheduled off-road riding due to construction work, and realised it had taken almost 3 months (compared to the 3 weeks I'd scheduled) to ride this incredible country

Chile

Dates in country	Sat 13-Thur 18 Mar and Fri 9-Sun 11 Apr
Number of days	8 (I made a number of sorties into Chile at various times, sometimes just for a few hours when passing through Tierra Del Fuego)
Population (millions)	16.5
Capital	Santiago
Area (km sq)	750,000
Currency	Chilean peso
Entry/exit points	South: Punta Delgada, El Turbio (nr Puerto Natales ferry to Puerto Montt); north: final exit from Argentina and entry into Chile at Paso De Jama, leaving Chile at Arica into Peru
Total distance miles (km)/date	27,921 (44,934)/Fri 9 Apr at Tocopilla
Average miles (km) per day	140 (225)
Accommodation	Backpacker hostel/hotel
Food	Excellent red wine (on a par with Argentina); fresh fruit and jam
Value	Good value accommodation and food
Rating (out of 10)	8

In a nutshell

Torres del Paine National Park is stunning. Earthquakes appear to be common. Friendly and generous people.

Route

After ducking in and out of Chile in Southern Patagonia the route north took in Puerto Natales, Punta Arenas, Puerto Montt (back into Argentina at Bariloche north to Salta), Calama, Tocopilla, Arica.

Rider notes

Bike – Following its service in Salta the bike was running well, although

Chile

Tocopilla
This simple Chilean fishing port had suffered a severe earthquake. Some buildings had been repaired and freshly painted in bright colours (as if to indicate a new start), whilst others remained dilapidated. The medical building (left) was just a fascia

Vibrant artwork brightened up the streets; the detail is amazing. This is the side of a house!

struggled a little on a long climb at altitude.
Maps – Producciones Carto Graficas/tourist road map.

Rider log
It was a huge ride to get to Tocopilla, Chile: 268 miles (430km) reaching 4800m (15,750 feet) above sea level at the peak of the ride, freezing first thing and baking by 11am. On arrival at the border crossing from Argentina

I struggled to remove a few layers, to the amusement of the border guards.

Saw lots of mining; scenery not great although Tocopilla was interesting, the shanty towns on its outskirts making it seem ramshackle, although it turns out there was an earthquake there two years previously from which it had not recovered. Imagine a 27,000 population fishing port crossed with a mining town that's been hit by a 7.7-on-the-Richter-Scale earthquake: no wonder it felt rough. The lovely, friendly people there – victims of the earthquake – made me regret my initial impression of their town.

Route 1 north runs right along the Oceano Pacifico coast (as it's named on local maps), and what an amazing road it is: the ocean with its huge surf to the left, mountains to the right, and hardly any traffic. I had to come inland from the coast and up and over the mountains on Route 5, riding along a mountain ridge into a gusty valley in the heat of the Atacama desert. I could feel myself starting to overheat so picked up the pace to try and generate a breeze, but it was like riding in the blast from a hairdryer. High in the mountains, the drop on one side of the road was the steepest I'd yet encountered, and the gust from a passing wagon threatened to have me over the edge. It's possible to look over the edge (no barriers) and see cars that have actually gone over, and memorials line the road: crosses and flags (sometimes red or the Chilean flag), a constant reminder to focus on the task in hand and keep it on the tarmac ...

Tocopilla to Arica
Coastal riding can't be beaten (above)

Racing sundown: get to towns before nightfall (left)

Friends in high places (inset)

Sat nav mapping was poor here; certainly within the towns, and Arica was no exception. Stopping to ask a local for directions in my broken Spanish, as always I dismounted and removed my helmet (after 300 miles in the searing heat this can be quite an effort, but is always worth it: imagine trying to talk to a local wearing a helmet and on the bike – no chance). As I removed my lid I could hear loud 'oink oink oink' noises, and wondered what the hell was making the noise as I couldn't see any pigs! As I looked around, all of a sudden I was covered in yoghurt-like gloop – me and the bike. The guy I'd stopped to ask directions from pointed skyward at massive birds roosting in palm trees. They'd only gone and crapped all over me! The locals were absolutely wetting themselves with laughter, although did get me a towel and wiped me clean, as well as my helmet, bike and luggage. The whole town and plaza was simply covered in guano; it was pretty grim.

It had been a really long day (341 miles/548km) at high altitude, and very hot. I parked up, found a hotel which charged me 20,000 pesos (£27) for the first night and 14,000 (£19) for the second, and had free underground parking (a bonus). There was a carnival on that night with dancing in the street, a parade the next morning, and a market in the afternoon. There was always something going on in South America and most towns have a strong community life.

Peru

Dates in country	Mon 12-Tue 20 Apr
Number of days	9
Population (millions)	28.5
Capital	Lima
Area (km sq)	1,285,000
Currency	Nuevo sol
Entry/exit points	From Chile at Arica/Tacna; exit into Ecuador at Macara
Total distance miles (km)/date	29,380 (47,282)/Fri 16 April
Average miles (km) per day	160 (257)
Accommodation	Hotel
Food	Chicken – if Argentina is steak, Peru is chicken. Pollo everywhere: dinner, tea and even breakfast. Huge chicken farms along the coast are never-ending
Value	Cheap, but quality of food and accommodation poor so not good value – brought my budget back into line here
Rating (out of 10)	6

In a nutshell
Not a country I'd rush back to, but interesting in a number of places. There seemed to be a lot of poverty, though towns became bigger and more difficult to navigate as I edged closer to Lima, which is reported as being 'difficult' to ride through.

Route
Moquegua, Camana, Nazca, Chilca, Casma, Trujillo, Chiclayo, Piura, Macara.

Rider notes
Beware of the dog! Wild dogs, that is, guarding gomeria (tyre repair places in the desert).
Bike – I had to keep checking the bike's air filter to clear it of sand.
Maps – Producciones Carto Graficas/tourist road map.

Rider log
I left Arica on Monday 12 April and made the short (30km/19 mile) journey to

cnt'd page 156

THE REAL WAY ROUND

Arica to Moquegua (opposite page & above)
The whole town felt very fresh – organic, almost – and probably is

Camana to Nazca (below)
Beach bums: surprisingly, there wasn't much activity on the beaches. The surf was incredible, though, and washed up some pretty big fish and mammals – dead and alive

THE REAL WAY ROUND

the Peruvian border, which was an efficient crossing with various paperwork and an official check of the bike's chassis and engine number.

Peru was mostly long stretches of desert riding, some desert valleys, and alongside the Pacific Ocean, the day's ride ending in either a nice, friendly town or one that was generally run-down. I came across a few friendly police check points where officers were only interested in the bike. No sat nav mapping but, to be fair, it's only one road straight up the coast, so able to get by using the compass occasionally and checking for signposts to Lima. The first town, Moquegua, was absolutely lovely: quiet and friendly, with markets and a number of cafés around the central square, and an all-important cash machine to withdraw funds for the rest of the country. I was intrigued by two guys sitting in the square, traditional typewriters clattering and bouncing on temporary tables as they typed prrofessional-looking letters for those who needed to correspond with official bodies – banks or the government, say. The customer dictated what they wanted, the chaps typed it, and then gave the customer the letter to post.

On this section of the journey the time zones kept going back an hour, and it was the second time in a week that I lived the same hour again, which can't be a bad thing! In China I kept losing time, which was not so good.

Queues for banks in South America are so long that they extend around the block; the only parallel I can draw is a queue at the ticket office for an important football cup clash. I never got to the bottom of why this happens, although no one seems to use the cash machines. Hmmm ...

The next day there was still a morning haze over the ocean when I left Camana for a great ride along the coast with massive sand dunes to the right, the Pacific Ocean to the left, and a few twisty bits thrown in as well. I rode through desert villages, valleys, and more farming land. The beaches were simply sensational (the best I've seen); huge surf stretching for miles. A massive dead seal lay on one beach, vultures perched on top, pecking away – not such a nice sight. Bright red crabs scuttled all over the beach, too.

Camana to Nazca *(below & top right)*
Moquegua to Camana *(middle right)*
Chiclayo to Macara *(bottom right)*

Long, desert, coastal roads; calls for 'social change,' and advertising for refreshing 'Inca Kola'

Peru

I got lots of friendly waves and honks from truck drivers as I rode, but didn't see another bike all that day. After a 250-mile (400km) ride, I found a great little place to stay in a town called Nazca (famous for Nazca Lines, a series of ancient geoglyphs) behind which I was able to store my bike that evening. Total mileage 28,855 (46,437km); so far so good in Peru.

I made a blunder on my first day in the country by taking out too much cash at the first ATM, as I was worried whether there would be cash machines in the smaller villages along the coast. I didn't realise that everythig would be so cheap: Peru is the cheapest country I visited since some of the smaller villages in China.

A couple of days later in Chilca I woke feeling ill, and vomited until my stomach was empty. I didn't want to move as I felt so ill, but decided I couldn't stay as the hotel was very poor and the stench from the toilet made me feel even worse. Even sticking my head out of the window to try and get some fresh air didn't help as all I could smell was chicken from the chicken farms that are everywhere along the coast, in amongst all the massive sand dunes. The best thing for me to do was pack up and get out quickly.

I went downstairs to say cheerio to the owner – who was eating a plate of chips and rice at 7.30 in the morning – and he decided that he'd like to look at my photographs. As he stood up to shake my hand his pants fell down. Crying with laughter, and wondering what on earth was going on, I got on my bike and left. I was out of Chilca – thank God – but nervous about the run through Lima later the same morning.

Approaching the city I was waved through a couple of toll booths without incident. Three lanes of traffic heading into the city increased first to four lanes, and then five, with buses stopping wherever and whenever they wanted, and mini vans and trike taxis cutting everyone up in a bid to be the first to get the passengers. It reminded me of a relay race where athletes jockey and scramble to pass the baton and be first away. It was hectic, but this was the only issue.

Exiting Lima absolutely drained I was stopped by the police. I muttered that I didn't speak much Spanish but the officer's attention was already on another motorist he'd pulled over. After ten minutes of standing around, waiting in the blistering heat I asked did he want anything from me or could I go? I was told I could go. This made me really angry, as he'd made me wait around for nothing, and I was just so hot. It wasn't yet 11.30 in the morning and I'd already had several wacky experiences: probably an average day, there, though.

Continuing north up the coast I went through a little town, and was again waved over by two officers in a jeep. Feigning ignorance I carried on,

Chilca to Casma
Typical Peruvian street eaterie, although 'restaurant' was probably pushing it a bit ...

THE REAL WAY ROUND

Camana to Nazca (left)

Chiclayo to Macara (above & below)

Sandstorms (of which there were plenty) made the ride difficult in places as sand drifts covered the roads – and me! Windswept desert villages were a common sight

only to look in my mirror and see that the jeep was following me, so I admitted defeat and pulled over. Apparently, I'd gone through a red light, the fine for which one of the officers wrote on a piece of paper: $100! (£60). After abject apologies and some negotiation I gave him the equivalent of about £20 in local currency to get him off my case, and, as I remounted, they were laughing together at how easily I'd paid up. I was feeling so drained that all I wanted was to find somewhere to stay so continued to my destination town of Casma.

En route I suddenly felt a massive pain in my thigh, like a jabbing feeling. I immediately stopped and discovered that a wasp had flown into the air vents I'd cut in my trousers in Indonesia when it was so hot. Getting him out I could see he'd made a bit of a mess of my thigh, which was pretty painful and irritated.

Further down the road, about 50 miles (80km) north of Lima, a thunderstorm blew up. It was the worst yet, with wind whipping up from the coast and visibility down to five metres (5.5 yards). Sand rained down and around, battering me, and when I got off the bike there was sand on the seat, sand in my pants and all over the place. It was quite scary riding in it as there were wagons coming towards me, and all I could do was follow the edge of the road for the next mile or so (2km). My face was bright red from sandblast and sunburn.

Casma to Huanchaco
Unique Peruvian reed fishing boats, caballitos de totora, which have been used for the last 3000 years – and a very skillful fisherman

Arriving in Casma (275 miles (442km) – total mileage 29,275 (47,113km) – I went to the pharmacy about my wasp sting and was given antihistamine and cream. The pharmacist also wanted to give me an injection, but after what I'd seen in Peru I wasn't keen on using needles, and thought "I'll stick with the cream, thanks."

I found some decent digs where I could store the bike. I was relieved that my passage through Lima had gone well as I was dreading getting stuck in the city. I estimated I could be out of Peru in four or five days: I was going to go to Cusco and do Machu Picchu but decided to stay on the coast instead, from which I think I got a real feel for Peru. It's not a place I would revisit as it's pretty rough, and much of it seems to be either under construction or poverty-stricken. There's a lot of dirt, and the heat and desert conditions are draining, making rehydration sachets a necessity on numerous occasions.

I met a couple from Leeds who were cycling tandem through South America, from Ushuaia to Cartagena. They were good people to talk to and compare notes with, and generally have a laugh about what we'd encountered on the road. Tim carried pebbles in the back of his jacket to fend off the wild dogs who, driven by hunger, sometimes try and take chunks out of travellers.

On my final day in Peru, heading north on the 'Panamerican Norte' (road 1N), just before Piura I saw water being delivered to the people. Outside every little house waited big containers, or buckets with plastic over the top outside the poorer abodes.

As I turned east the landscape became greener due to irrigation from the mountains. My last memory of Peru was of how green it was in the north compared to further south on the coastal desert roads – why would people choose to live in such harsh desert conditions, I wondered? I stopped for lunch at an amazing little café where the beer was being delivered under armed guard, and meat and fish hung on a washing line, waiting to be cooked on a wood-fuelled stone furnace, from which dangled various pots. An incredibly basic setup but the food was fantastic. It made me think about the excess that we have in England and developed countries: does anyone really need the Perfect Pancake Maker available to buy on a TV shopping channel?

Peru was so cheap I was able to get my spending back on track. I'd withdrawn 1200 sol (just under £300) on the first day, and had expected to need more, but I still had just over 500, which meant I had enough to replace my sunglasses yet again. This time I put them on the back of the bike whilst I was taking a photo, and rode off with them still there. As they fell to the road, I glanced in my mirror and saw a car drive over them ...

Chiclayo to Macara
This top bloke suggested we might part-exchange our transportation, and I couldn't help noticing that the profile of the mule was very similar to that of the Ténéré. Where did Yamaha engineers get their inspiration from, I wonder ...?

Ecuador

Dates in country	Wed 21-Sun 25 April
Number of days	5
Population (millions)	14
Capital	Quito
Area (km sq)	283,500
Currency	US dollar
Entry/exit points	From Peru at Macara. Exit into Colombia at Ipiales
Total distance miles (km)/date	30,172 (48,557)/Fri 23 April
Average miles (km) per day	90 (145)
Accommodation	Hotels
Food	Pork – spit-roasted pigs everywhere – delicious, with plenty of crackling
Value	Good; standards usually very high
Rating (out of 10)	8

In a nutshell
Mountain riding with some cloud; wonderful people (many different cultural groups); good food in the villages.

Route
Macara, Cuenca, Riobamba, Ibarra.

Rider notes
Bike – Nothing to report. Had to pay for underground parking in Cuenca for a few days as no parking in the city.
Maps – Simple tourist map.

Rider log
I left Chiclayo in Peru very early on the morning of Tuesday 20 April, and continued north to a place called Piura, which is close to the border. Riding east a little way inland to get away from the coast (I'd had enough coastal deserts to last me a lifetime), I took the more scenic route into Ecuador,

Chiclayo to Macara
Welcome to Ecuador

Chiclayo to Macara
Riding in the clouds, and mountain workers encountered there. The farmer appears to be wearing a couple of his flock ...

arriving at the border crossing town of Macara at 2.30 in the afternoon. The officials were quite busy, the Peruvian Customs officer insisting on finishing the letter he was typing before he would look at my documents (and military officers are not very quick at typing; trust me). Passing into Ecuador all of the officials were watching the Champions League, which they dragged their attention away from long enough to stamp the paperwork, before refocussing on the match.

A night in Macara was followed by twisty, simply sensational mountain roads, which zigzagged in and out of cloud and green farming valleys. The lower-altitude valleys were hot, and the mountains refreshingly cool at 2-3000 metres (6500-9800 feet). Lovely green valleys housed lots of little villages, all amazingly different, their inhabitants wearing various types of traditional dress. In one village, everyone was dressed in black from head to toe: even the kids wore black hats. There are 16 different ethnic groups in Ecuador and it wasn't long before I saw two or three whilst on the road.

I arrived in Cuenca Canton – a really friendly town – on Friday 23 April after a 247-mile (400km) ride, taking total mileage to 30,161 (48,539km). Cuenca Canton's population of around 400,000 feature

cnt'd page 165

Macara to Cuenca Canton
Stunning scenery and magnificent cities

Ecuador

Chiclayo to Macara   Opposite ends of the Yamaha scale   **Macara to Cuenca Canton**

Cuenca Canton
Hats off to these chaps – what a skill! – I could have watched them for hours

Cuenca Canton
'Barrow girls' wheeled fruit and veg into Cuenca Canton from nearby villages

Cuenca Canton
Best to keep on top of kit maintenance en route: a good clean and polish and my boots were like new after 30,000 miles

a mix of dress codes: some ladies wear white hats with a black band that resemble a trilby, and bright dresses, and all carry young children on their backs. A stomach upset meant a few days off the bike, during which I hatched a plan to get to Calgary. Shipping the bike from Calgary to London would cost around £1500: I'd have preferred it to be less but, with only a few months left, time was at a premium. As it was, I would have to ride about 700 miles (1126km) a week for the next 10 weeks.

After leaving Cuenca Canton I started to climb again, riding at 3500m (11,500 feet) straight into thick cloud and low visibility (5-10m/16-30 feet), and wet – not rain, just moisture at altitude. I got behind a car that was doing

Cuenca Canton to Riobamba
Bacon Bap – and then some! This idea would go down a storm in any English biker café. The soup was amazing, too: you won't go hungry riding in Ecuador (and overleaf)

THE REAL WAY ROUND

a decent speed and used it as a buffer for oncoming vehicles and cliffside edges. In the mountains women at roadside cafes roasted pigs, using a device something like a Bunsen burner to remove hair and crisp the skin.

Further up the road I stopped near to where an old guy was farming. He was wearing these amazing sheepskin pads to protect his legs, and his wife wore traditional jewellery and hat: they both looked fabulous and were super-friendly. They wanted dollars but I had only bananas so I gave them a couple. We tried to communicate, and I grabbed a couple of photos – great people with amazing stories – wished I could speak Spanish!

A break in the clouds revealed stunning scenery and blue skies as I kind of skirted round the mountains. Ecuador was beautiful: the people were great and the traditional dress amazing; such a refreshing change from Peru (sorry to all Peruvians).

I headed for Ibarra, some 206 miles (330km) distant, which brought total mileage to 30,533 (49,138km). Ibarra was a real surprise: I knew I was getting towards the Caribbean but the influence was such that I got a real sense of the people, dress and food of this colourful part of the world. Just before the Colombian border the group of brightly-dressed women carrying pots on their heads could have been a scene from Jamaica (not that I've ever been!).

Colombia

Dates in country	Mon 26 April–Mon 10 May
Number of days	14
Population (millions)	44
Capital	Bogota
Area (km sq)	1,138,000
Currency	Colombian peso
Entry/exit points	From Ecuador at Ipiales. Exit into Panama at Tocumen airport, Bogota
Total distance miles (km)/date	31,410 (50,549)/Fri 30 April
Average miles (km) per day	102 (164): the best rides of the trip
Accommodation	Hotels
Food	Excellent coffee – who needs food? – and equally good soups (which was a surprise)
Value	Excellent
Rating (out of 10)	10: Incredible – have promised myself I will return!

In a nutshell
Colombia and Indonesia were my joint top favourite countries as they have everything. Ignore the hype about drug traffickers and muggings: Colombia rocks!

Route
Pasto, Popayán, La Pintada, Turbo, Cartagena, Taganga, Aguachica, San Gil, Bogota.

Rider notes
Bike – Oil change in Cartagena.
Maps – *Guia de Rutas por Colombia* – local pack with maps and guides celebrating 10 years of tourism.

Rider log
A curvy mountain road through numerous fruit farms took me to the border for one of the simplest crossings of the whole trip that took just 45 minutes,

THE REAL WAY ROUND

Ibarra to Pasto
Colombian colours and countryside

including changing a small amount of money with the cambio guys. 'Cambio' is Spanish for 'change' and it's usual at borders to find men who, for a small percentage, will exchange currencies for you, so that you at least have sufficient funds to get to an ATM. Additionally, I paid one guy an extra dollar to look after my bike whilst I dealt with Customs, paperwork, etc. At every border I found fixers, currency exchangers, parking assistants and general helpers: all come at a price, of course, but sometimes this is a sound investment. Altogether a friendly experience which resulted in all items getting stamped and a 60-day Colombian visa.

140 miles (225km) later I arrived in Pasto, with a total mileage of 30,673 (49,363km) after the first day in Colombia. The scenery was stunning and Pasto had everything a first-stop town needs – cash machine for local currency, bookshop to buy an excellent map – *Guia de Rutas por Colombia* – celebrating the 10-year anniversary of tourism, and a café for coffee, sandwich and cake.

A little nerve-wracking was being offered certain 'services' by girls, who obviously spotted me a mile off, despite my fond belief that I blended in with the locals. The ladies operated alongside telephone card sales people and Panini World Cup sticker stands (the entire England team for 5000 pesos (£1.80): swapsies not necessary here as packs were split to allow collectors to buy only those stickers they needed). And it was only just gone ten in the morning ...

On the way to Popayán – the next town, some 156 miles (250km) north – mountainous roads were slow and windy. A truck had completely rolled over on one, whilst a group of people at the edge of a bank were the passengers who had scrambled from a bus that had gone over the edge (something I last saw in Indonesia). The temptation to stop was strong but my experience had taught me it was probably best to avoid fraught situations such as this. Popayán was a complete contrast to Pasto: a university town with a lovely colonial square – Parque de Caldas – and white, clean, simply immaculate buildings. The other side of town, however, was a different story. Really rough, I witnessed a lad inhale from a piece of foil and immediately collapse, just as if his legs had been cut from under him – God knows what it was he inhaled but it must have been phenomenally strong. I turned on my heel and walked straight back to the hostel: finding yourself in the wrong part of town usually means trouble – wherever you are in the world.

I by-passed Cali through some industrial-scale farmland complete with huge harvesting machines, and labour forces being mini-bussed about: not much tradition here. Route 25, which follows the River Cauca, has nothing apart from roadside knocking shops: I kept riding. It was beginning to get dark, and I was just starting to worry that I'd left it too late to find somewhere to stay when I spotted the sign for Hotel La Pintada – what a relief!

I loved Colombia. It might be a little bit edgy in parts, but this does

Colombia

Ibarra to Pasto

This young lad was ploughing a small patch of land next to the road, hanging on to the back of the plough as it cut through the rugged earth. It was a great moment, and he was a really nice kid as well. His dad wanted me to marry his daughter; he actually brought her to me, which was a bit embarrassing. She was incredibly pretty, too, but she ran off and hid somewhere. Welcome to Colombia

have a positive side as it has loads of energy, and the landscape is stunningly beautiful. The ride was great; really interesting and enjoyable.

There were a great many mopeds on the roads – in South America more than anywhere (probably equal to Indonesia) – but also some decent-sized bikes knocking about. My number plate had fallen off so I strapped it back on with tape. I also copied the locals after being stopped a couple of times by putting the registration number on my helmet with stickers. In fact, this is a legal requirement after a spate of drive-by shootings were carried out by men using mopeds as getaway bikes. All riders have the registration number on their helmet and hi-vis jacket so that they can be identified.

One of the best rides of the trip

I arrived at Turbo at about six in the evening, completely knackered after leaving La Pintada at around 8.30 that morning, and riding with very few stops when I realised I either needed to make up some time or be left in the middle of nowhere. In a single day I think I saw everything that epitomises Colombia.

After finding somewhere to stay, in the morning, clouds sat in the valley that my room overlooked; it was a great place, somewhere you could easily spend a week. The road out of La Pintada was pretty minor, and continued alongside the River Cauca for about 60 miles (100km), which was lovely. Guys wearing cowboy hats were moving cattle around the hillsides on

THE REAL WAY ROUND

horseback. At a small school I spotted all of the kids were waving and playing, so I stopped to chat with their teacher and take some photos, which was fun.

After a town called Santa Fe de Antioquia, the road split into two mountain passes which made for slow going deep into the jungle, especially as the road was bad. The day was dominated by checkpoints with a strong military presence – tanks and heavily-armoured vehicles were the norm. Initially, a couple of soldiers stopped me, though, after that, I was getting the thumbs up as if it had been radioed through that a mad English biker was on his way. They told me that Turbo was still five hours away – it was 2pm – and the last thing I wanted was to be stuck in the jungle overnight. Although everyone had been friendly I didn't want to risk an impromptu stopover in an area with such a high military presence, which is there for a reason.

I rode through some dodgy places on the way to Turbo; one town, Dabeiba (population about 10,000), had a 'Welcome to Dabeiba' sign, which seemed at complete odds with the soldiers and hardware on show there. Nevertheless, because the area felt tense and edgy, the military presence was reassuring. The afternoon was passing quickly and the fear of being stranded overnight between towns or checkpoints made me ride hard, despite the poor road surface, especially in the jungle sections.

I encountered a number of checkpoints en route, and one in particular stands out in my memory, as half of the 20 or so young soldiers gathered round the bike, asking questions, which was a bit worrying initially, although all ended in a friendly fashion. The towns I passed through became smaller and the people there would stop, look and point at me and the bike as we passed. I carried on through Turbo as I couldn't see anywhere to stay the night, and made it to the coast just before dusk, where I found some beach-type jungle huts/bungalows to rent at a small village called Simona del Mar. I was extremely relieved to stop: it was late; getting dark, and an injury I'd sustained earlier when a wasp had got inside my helmet, attached itself to my face, and stung me just above my left eye – ouch – had become quite painful. Lesson learnt, though: don't ride through farmland – where bugs, flies, butterflies, and wasps are more prolific – with your visor up!

All-in-all it had been an interesting day with the ranch guys, military, school, and the stunning ride through coffee and banana plantations, amazing scenery, the road to myself and checkpoint fun and games – incredible. In hindsight I would love to ride this route again, but spend more time in and around the smaller towns, though there are some I would not want to stay in on my own. The sight of all the military – guys in full camouflage sat in the jungle with machine guns – was just amazing, though I did wonder why they were there in such number: general security or to keep control of certain groups? I'd seen it all during this ride in north western Colombia and loved every minute – it was a key moment in the trip and felt special – I only wish I had stopped overnight in the Santa Fe area and carried on the following morning to give myself more time to enjoy the amazing jungle rainforest.

Night-time was noisy with the sounds of animals in the jungle, and pitch black. Though exhausted I couldn't sleep as I remained tense and nervous, aware of my isolation. The realisation, as on many other nights when laying down to sleep, that no one knew where I was should anything bad happen was not conducive to sweet dreams …

I'd ridden 286 miles (460km) that day through some pretty tough conditions, though thankfully no rain as that would have finished me off. Total mileage 31,391 (50,518km) on Monday 3 May.

Colombia

I hit the outskirts of Cartagena early evening the next day. I had to find a certain hostel that dealt with shipping to Panama, and had storage for the bike, but a weird moped rider pointed his finger at me as if firing a gun, so I pulled into a busy service station and hired a cab to lead me to the hostel. This turned out to be a very good move following a long day's ride ending in an unfamiliar city because the town was hard to navigate, and well worth the 5000 pesos charge.

Despite making numerous trips over the next few days to the marina and scouting around, the crossing to Panama that would circumnavigate the Darian Gap (dense jungle between Colombia and Panama, with no road) didn't come off. There was one offer from Leonardo, an Italian captain (accompanied by his wife: 25, Colombian, and heavily pregnant) and his

Pasto to Popayán
The streets were always lively: military in Popayan; community bands in Cartagena, and fruit and veg stalls everywhere

THE REAL WAY ROUND

Pasto to Popayán *(main);* ***La Pintada to Turbo*** *(inset, top);* ***Turbo to Cartagena*** *(inset, middle);* ***Cartagena to Taganga*** *(inset, bottom)*
Spectacular scenery; challenging roads, and strange road signs. Note the bike's reg number stickered to my helmet

daughter), who had recently had his boat robbed and then been mugged by neighbours of his wife's family during a visit. He told me he feared for his life. The passengers – a transvestite Brazilian biker, an Argentinian biker, three Americans, two other English guys and me – needed to make the crossing worthwhile for Leonardo in terms of money, but he didn't trust the Brazilian, and kept asserting that all bikes and baggage would be checked

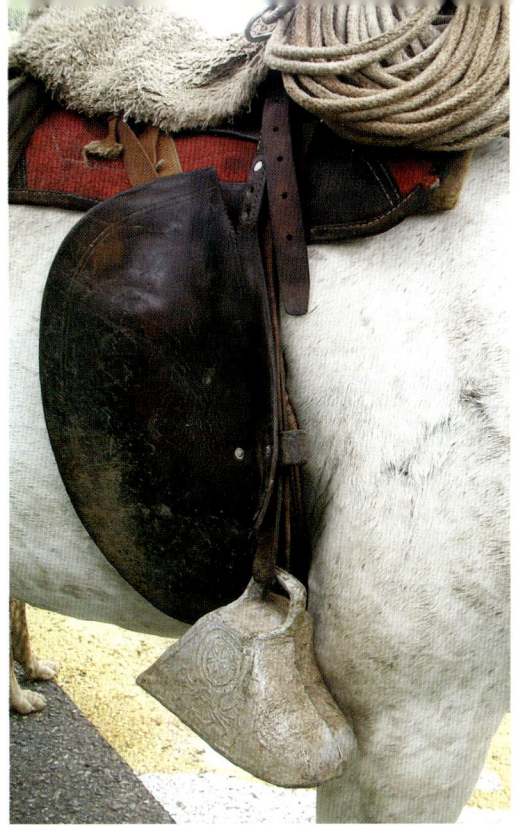  

La Pintada to Turbo
The people of Colombia are very warm; ignore the stories about drugs and crime. Everyone was very friendly, from cowboys in the street to kids in village schools

by Customs with sniffer dogs, doing this so often that, eventually, it spooked the Americans, who pulled out the following morning, making the voyage unviable. Looking back I laugh when I think about this farcical scene, but at the time it was frustrating. High tension moments are sometimes some of the most memorable.

I managed to change the bike's oil, which would give me another 4000 miles (6437km) and get me to the United States, and set off to Bogota the following day to fly over the Darian Gap on 11 May. Bogota is actually 2500 metres (8202 feet) above sea level, which I didn't expect, and it's quite high around the mountains on the edge of the city. It cost about $1000 to ship the bike from Bogota to Panama.

A Colombian football match that I watched on TV was certainly not for the faint-hearted. Apparently, fans can be so violent that police use shields to protect a player taking a corner from missiles thrown by spectators – a very collectable Panini sticker if you can find it!

Bogota International Airport: 8am Monday 10 May
A full day of paperwork with Lyn Cargo agents Oscar and Alvedo included two police checks of the bike, complete with sniffer dog – a lovely Golden Labrador – which made me nervous as hell. The bike was obviously clean, and I don't touch drugs, but a lot of the chaps in the backpacker hostels dabble, and you never know what might have touched the bike when it was left overnight.

It was evident that Colombia doesn't employ the same aviation rules as other countries, as I didn't have to disconnect the battery or pack it down, just pay for the weight of the bike (they weren't concerned about actual size as there was room on the plane). Leaving the bike there, I got a lift back to the hostel on the back of one of the freight company guy's moped, which was interesting. He weaved quickly through some really tight, night-time Bogota traffic: no speedo, no rev counter, dim lights, but hammering through the narrowest of gaps between buses, wagons and cars.

Alarm set for 5am the next morning – Panama here I come!

Tank bag notes
Place names; points of reference (Apartado has a small airport); total mileage

THE REAL WAY ROUND

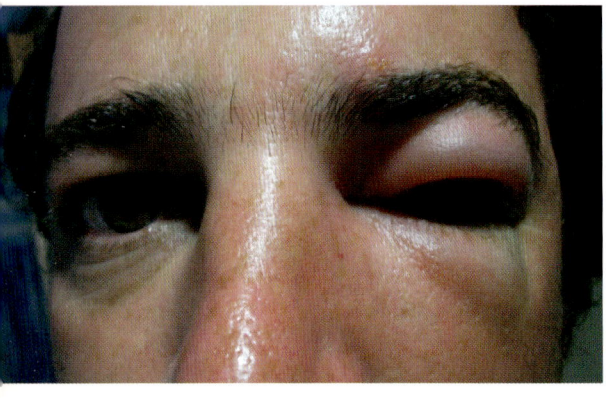 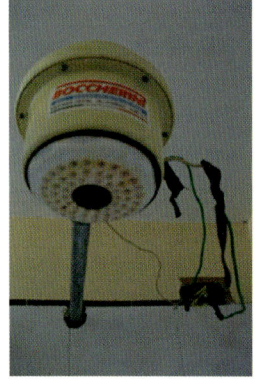

Pasto to Popayán
There are some hazards on a trip like this. 1) wasps and other insects that get inside clothing and helmet and sting ... 2) ... and probably the most dangerous shower in the world: electric wires taped together to power the element and heat the water

Cartagena
Regular oil changes and coffee breaks will help get you and your bike around the world; interestingly, a similar pouring action is required for both

Colombia

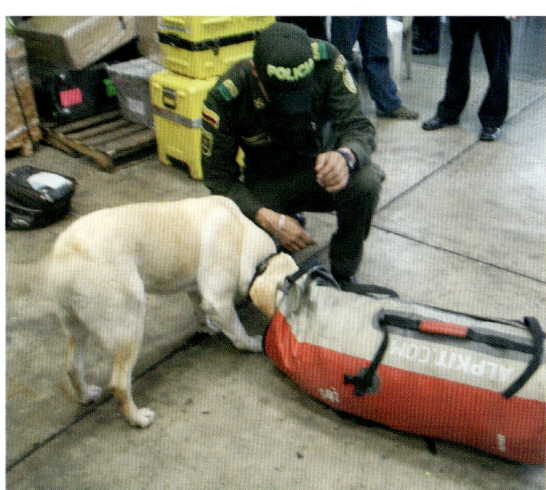

Bogota
Arranging to freight the bike meant jumping through a few hoops: safety; paperwork; Customs, contraband searches; bike checks, and more ...

175

Panama

Dates in country	*Tue 11-Fri 14 May*
Number of days	*4*
Population (millions)	*3*
Capital	*Panama City*
Area (km sq)	*78,000*
Currency	*US dollar/balboa*
Entry/exit points	*From Bogota, Colombia flight to Tocumen. Exit into Costa Rica at Paso Canoas*
Total distance miles (km)/date	*32,898 (54,944)/Fri 14 May*
Average miles (km) per day	*110 (177)*
Accommodation	*Hotel*
Food	*Spicy fried chicken with rice and vegetables*
Value	*Good, but I expect prices to rise as tourism increases*
Rating (out of 10)	*9*

Air waybill for the Ténéré

In a nutshell
Amazing beaches and rainforest – a really pleasant surprise; tourism in its infancy.

Route
Tocumen airport, Rio Hato, David, Guadalupe.

Rider notes
Bike – Nothing to report other than that the Ténéré loved the twisty bits in the mountains before Costa Rica near Parque Nacional Volcan Baru.
Maps – *Nelles Map Central America*.

Rider log
My flight landed in Panama (Tocumen airport) at 9.30 in the morning, although the bike didn't arrive there until 4pm due to a delay with the cargo section. Because the bike was late, I booked into a hotel near the airport US$99/£63 (ouch! – the most expensive hotel of the trip), though benefits

Panama

Tocumen
Welcome to Panama

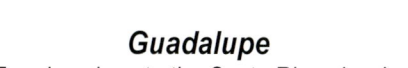

Guadalupe
Farming close to the Costa Rican border

included breakfast, pool, WiFi, and free shuttle bus to the airport, which I had to use three times. Finally got the bike at around half six that evening so the decision to enjoy a little luxury was a good one as it was too late to ride.

Unfortunately, Panamanian Customs don't recognise the Carnet de Passage, and completes its own temporary import documentation. The young lad doing it couldn't work out the difference between UK and England, despite my trying to explain a number of times. To be fair to him it does say 'United Kingdom, Great Britain and Northern Ireland' on the passport, whilst other paperwork states 'England.' Confusion reigned until his KFC delivery arrived, whereupon he filled in a few gaps on the form by hand, stamped everything, shoved the papers at me and waved me out with one hand whilst peeling the lid off his bucket with the other – good ol' Colonel Sanders and his secret recipe!

Two currencies are used in Panama – the balboa and the US dollar – and US influence is massively obvious after South America, which, in the main, doesn't seem to appreciate US exports (and why would it?), and is the better for it. In Panama, however, KFC, McDonalds and pizza chains are rife, their advertising billboards much in evidence at the side of the road.

I rode from Tocumen to the beaches of Rio Hato for a couple of nights to just hang out, and witnessed the early morning return of fisherman who had been out all night: their catch – whopping sharks – in the boats. A woman waiting on the beach was picked up by the boats which then went some 20 metres (65 feet) offshore whilst she cut off the fins and gutted the fish with a huge machete, throwing fins and innards back into the sea. The boats were bringing in about eight sharks each, which would, no doubt, shock environmentalists, but if this is their livelihood it's hard to comment without knowing the background and any alternatives.

I tried to find the Panama Canal but gave up as I got lost. The heat was intense, in any case, and no doubt there would be tourists all over the place. Anyway, the Manchester Ship Canal takes some beating.

From Rio Hato, a 252 mile/405km ride on Friday (total mileage 32,877/52,910km) took me to Guadalupe, which has beautiful rainforest, and is within spitting distance of the border with Costa Rica that I intended to cross the next day.

The border between Panama and Costa Rica has three crossing points (top, middle, bottom), and I chose the middle one (Rio Sereno) where the Aduana (Customs) office was closed for the afternoon (they would process me but not the bike). Instead, I rode south and crossed at

THE REAL WAY ROUND

Paso Canoas, which is a much bigger border crossing. The lack of organisation at borders was becoming increasingly irritating, despite knowing I had only a few left to get through. No one appears to know what they are doing, added to which is the language barrier, queues and heat. Not getting across until four that afternoon meant I had to get a wiggle on to reach Dominical, Costa Rica before nightfall (total mileage 33,050/52,188).

Tocumen to Rio Hato
Returning from night fishing

Costa Rica

Dates in country	Sat 15-Mon 24 May
Number of days	10
Population (millions)	4
Capital	San Jose
Area (km sq)	51,000
Currency	Colón
Entry/exit points	From Panama at Paso Canoas. Exit into Nicaragua at Peñas Blancas
Total distance miles (km)/date	33,454 (53,838)/Fri 21 May
Average miles (km) per day	50 (80)
Accommodation	Hotel
Food	Touristy – the Americans love this place – therefore food good but slightly sanitised; not as good as the rest of Central America
Value	Prices good but highest in Central America due to tourism
Rating (out of 10)	8

In a nutshell
Volcanoes; jungles; beaches and surf.

Route
Along the coast to Dominical, mountain pass to San Jose, Arenal Volcano, Bahia de Salinas.

Rider notes
Some heavy rain; a series of short rides and 2-night stopovers.
Bike – Even fully loaded and two-up, the Ténéré took everything in its stride.
Maps – *Nelles Map Central America*.

Rider log
It was a straight run along the Pacific coastline to Dominical, which is

THE REAL WAY ROUND

Paso Canoas to Dominical
Obviously a serious police report – but what did it say?

Dominical to San Jose
Misty mountain roads with poor visibility, and poor road surface

essentially a surfing beach and small town. However, despite the short journey I was stopped by the police, though not sure why. The handwritten report (two pages of A4) took about 30 minutes to complete, and I received a souvenir carbon copy but no fine. I did wonder what I might be letting myself in for when I was asked to sign the document, but I was keen to get moving.

The next day I rode to the capital, San Jose (total mileage 33,158/53,362km), to meet a friend who was visiting for a week, during which time we pottered around the coastal rainforests and volcanic parks: Arenal Volcano is still active and at night it's possible to see the red lava spitting out the top of it.

The ride from Arenal Volcano to Jaco was done in huge thunderstorms: the weather had really deteriorated, giving rise to poor visibility and inches-deep water on the road. Parking up on the outskirts of Jaco to get my bearings, I'd just put the bike on the side stand when everything began to move: of course, an earthquake. Even the locals looked shocked as the buildings and trees swayed, creating a very strange sensation.

That night I stayed in Bahia de Salinas, a very quiet town that's famous for kite surfing, but which also has a lovely bay for walking and relaxing; four species of monkey that can be seen all over, and an amazing number of bright red crabs on the beach. Apart from tourism, agriculture and fishing are the town's other main industries. Before crossing into Nicaragua the next day the French owner of the Kite Surfing School advised me to get as far north as I could because a tropical storm was heading toward the south coast of Central America. This would be no easy task as the roads further north were only minor, and doing this meant quite a diversion in any case. An early start was called for so that I could weigh up my options ...

Arenal Volcano
Good scenery; volcanoes; flora and fauna

Nicaragua & Honduras

	Nicaragua	Honduras
Dates in country	Tue 25-Thur 27 May	Fri 28 May
Number of days	3	1
Population (millions)	5.5	7.5
Capital	Managua	Tegucigalpa
Area (km sq)	130,000	112,100
Currency	Gold córdoba	Lempira
Entry/exit points	From Costa Rica at Peñas Blancas/Somotillo	Goascoran into El Salvador
Total distance miles (km)/date	33,925 (54,597)/Thur 27 May	33,996 (54,711)/Fri 28 May
Average miles (km) per day	60 (96)	75 (120)
Accommodation	Hotel	Hotel
Food	Beef and rice	I remember a very spicy breakfast in particular!
Value	Excellent	Good
Rating (out of 10)	7	6

In a nutshell
Couldn't really get into the riding zone due to the carnage left by the storms.

Route
Nicaragua: Rivas, Granada, León; Honduras: Choluteca, Nacaome.

Rider notes
Bike – Difficult riding conditions due to Tropical Storm Agatha.

Maps – *Nelles Map Central America*.

Rider log
The border crossing into Nicaragua was a mud bath: a combination of deep potholes and hundreds of trucks producing slippery conditions that put me in mind of mud wrestling! I ended up paying a bloke on the Costa Rican side $10 (£6) to queue-jump, which worked, so thinking "what the hell" I

Bahia Salinas to Granada
The border crossing into Nicaragua was choked by heavy freight and a mud bath

THE REAL WAY ROUND

Bahia Salinas to Granada
Another part-exchange opportunity? At least it was a bike this time, though, having said that, I would probably take the mule from Peru in preference (although I liked the chrome tank)

Granada to León
The streets of León

León
Incredible images from the Museum of the Revolution (run by the revolutionaries themselves). It's not all historical, though, as city graffiti testifies

León
The owner of this stall stayed open late, hoping for a few last-minute sales

paid someone on the Nicaraguan side another $10/£7 to get me through Immigration and Customs quickly. It was quite usual at South and Central American border crossings for Customs officers to check over the bike, but the Nicaraguan officials took this a stage further and sterilised it (not very thoroughly), charging me $2 to do so, but then went on to sell me mandatory insurance ('tourism tax') for around $25/£16. What with this and the $20/£13 I'd already paid to queue-jump, it was quite an expensive crossing compared to others in South and Central America, but it was my choice to speed things up with a couple backhanders, so I can't complain.

Crossing the border the difference was immediately obvious. Nicaragua looks poorer, its farming, tin and wood shacks, the odd huge buffalo, and basic fruit and veg for sale at the roadside in direct contrast to the tourist attractions of Costa Rica. although it was a little more 'real' here I would say. Two lovely volcanoes greet you as you enter and ride west. It was absolutely chucking it down, though, which made me wonder whether it was worth continuing or to put in a 'big one' the next day.

I did continue, however, and the colonial town of Granada on the shores of Lake Nicaragua was my first stop, followed by a very wet ride to León. On the Thursday – May 27 – I didn't ride anywhere as the rain was just too heavy, increasing in intensity and flowing down the roads in streams. The day in León allowed me to catch up on general jobs and planning. The weather news wasn't good – it seemed the country was on the brink of a national disaster with rainfall of 185mm (over 7 inches) in just four hours in

THE REAL WAY ROUND

Nicaragua
News of Storm Agatha was extensively reported – and I was getting nervous

one city. In the rural areas it was worse, with people missing and communities devastated. News footage showed that the whole area was completely flooded after rivers burst their banks and roads were washed away, necessitating the evacuation of many by the military.

My plan of getting to Honduras the next morning didn't look at all feasible as the storm stretched along the coastline on the route I intended to take. News images of helicopters evacuating entire villages at risk of flooding – and landslides that had already occurred – were not encouraging. The already poor roads were in an absolute state: in patches the rain had lifted the tarmac, leaving just rubble. Floodwater pushed up drain covers, leaving them lying in the road and a hole where they should have been – extremely dangerous to try and negotiate. Despite all this turmoil, however, people seemed to get on with day-to-day stuff, certainly in and around the town of León, anyway.

The previous evening I'd eaten at a decent street café. A couple of times during my meal a kid had come up to the window asking for food, so I gave him some burger, which he ran off with and scoffed in seconds, as if he had not eaten for a week – which he probably hadn't. The next day I gave a kid some money, which I didn't usually do but, bugger it, what the hell. The Lonely Planet guide bangs on about not giving locals cash but I couldn't help it, as some of them look like they have absolutely nothing.

After waiting a couple of days in León for the weather to settle I eventually left to cross into Honduras, staying in a place called Choluteca (a midway point on the Honduran south coast). Due to the weather, road conditions and border crossing it took longer than usual to do a hundred miles (160km). Part of the road was under military control where it had flooded and was probably on the point of collapse. The destruction in and around Chinandega (the last town I rode through before leaving Nicaragua) and the level of flooding was terrible to see, with people desperately trying to recover their belongings from houses that were completely flooded. The shell shocked faces of displaced families walking about in a daze after losing their homes in the devastation, their belongings on their backs, brought a lump to my throat.

I spent only one night and day in Honduras and then continued on into El Salvador, determined to keep up the momentum despite the challenging conditions. Desperate for the rain to stop (everything was soaked but at least it was warm), I'd not seen blue sky for about ten days ...

León to Honduras border
Large-scale flooding meant catastrophe for the locals

Nicaraguan/Honduran border
At most borders in Central America it's possible and generally wise to spend about $10 (£6) on an 'assistant' (crossing fixer), who has knowledge of the process and various office locations. Try and remain patient, though; I was guilty of losing it at one border

El Salvador

Dates in country	Sat 29 May-Tue 2 June
Number of days	5
Population (millions)	7
Capital	San Salvador
Area (km sq)	21,000
Currency	US dollar
Entry/exit points	From Honduras at Santa Clara. Exit into Guatemala at Ahuachapan
Total distance miles (km)/date	34,118 (54,907)/Sat 29 May
Average miles (km) per day	70 (112)
Accommodation	Backpacker hostel
Food	Cheap but average quality, though plenty of choice from street vendors
Value	Very cheap
Rating (out of 10)	9

In a nutshell
Interesting history; poverty; good jungle walks but take a guide.

Route
Perquin, San Miguel, San Vicente (bypass San Salvador), Santa Ana, Juayua.

Rider notes
Bike – Watch out for post-storm landslides!

Maps – *Nelles Map Central America*.

Rider log
Finally, the sun appeared for a brief spell, causing the wet road to steam and my damp riding kit to very quickly become sauna-like, not helped by the fact that I began to sweat heavily: it was pretty unpleasant. Exiting the Honduras border, a payment of just $5 (£3) got me in the express lane (had I been over-paying previously?), but at the end of the process a further $15 (£9) was

THE REAL WAY ROUND

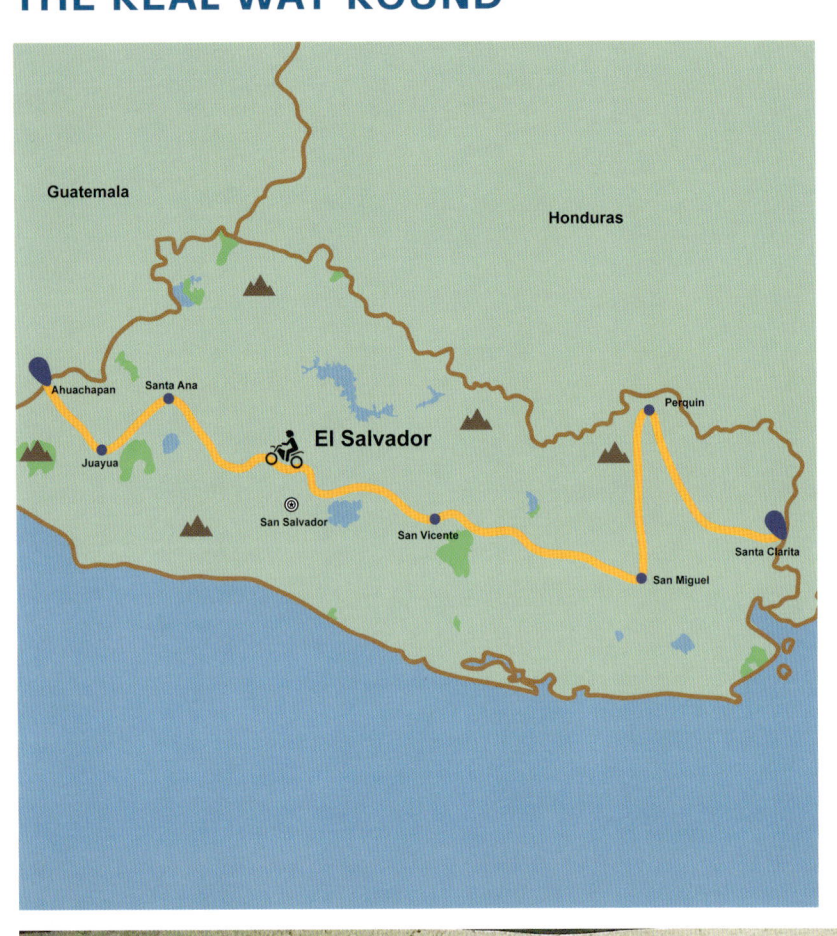

Santa Clara border
Smooth entry into El Salvador

Perquin to Juayua
Images from the museum at Perquin

El Salvador

demanded. By this time my patience at border crossings had been so sorely tested that I became visibly annoyed with the requests for money. It may have been unwise but, through tiredness, I just lost it and pushed my way through the queue to the office, where my passport and other documentation was, and gave the guy there a piece of my mind. Surprised, he dumped my papers and ran off as he knew he was about to get a rocket from the officers for taking liberties. Usually, the officials let these guys get on with it, as it makes the processing quicker and easier for all the staff, but taking it too far results in complaints which they don't like.

It was a short ride across a bridge to the El Salvador Immigration

Perquin to Juayua
Storm front. Tropical Storm Agatha had a massive impact along the southern coast of Central America. Flood defences were teetering, and landslides and flood water made a number of roads impassable

Juayua
Juayua is stunning: it's been given a complete makeover, and buildings, lampposts, and bins are brightly painted ...

Offices, but as Aduana (Customs) Officials were on a go-slow, I didn't get away until 2.45pm, despite arriving over two hours previously. I was stopped by the police later the same day so produced a copy of my driving licence, which they then demanded $45/£28 for the return of. By this point in my trip I'd become a little more self-assured – and also lost patience with all the scams – so I told him to keep it: a sharp contrast to my response to the young policemen in Ukraine.

I came to rest that day in the mountains of Perquin, 25 miles/40km north of the main Pan American Highway. Where I stayed was fabulous but the combination of it gettng dark early, very wet conditions, and a power cut

... although, on the edge of town, not all of the houses are as brightly decorated

made for an early night. The rain had returned, the resultant storm significant enough to be christened 'Storm Agatha.' The first storm of the tropical season, this was a devastating weather front of low pressure.

Perquin's Museum of the Revolution was basic but interesting, home to the usual posters and photographs, makeshift weaponry, and lots of anti-American paraphernalia. In fact, the museum's austerity somehow gave it more impact, helped by the fact that the guys who run it are ex-guerilla fighters from the Civil War that occurred between 1979 and 1992. One of the images from 1986 shows what look like kids facing soldiers in a standoff. When I remember '86 I think of the World Cup hosted by Mexico; just one country away from where these battles were fought.

Perquin to Juayua was 190 miles (305km) of absolutely awful conditions, with rivers and bridges compromised, and military and Red Cross (or equivalent) swinging into action. One massive dam was under severe pressure judging by the frantic activity and large number of locals watching events unfold. Water was coming through the bottom of the dam (possibly a controlled flow, but maybe not). I kept on riding.

Further west the rain began to subside and I managed to put in some decent miles (avoiding occasional landslides; in particular a huge one east of the capital) to get to Juayua. It was a tough ride with mudslides, lots of debris on the road, and locals out and about surveying the damage. The internet reported at least 200 people dead; more missing, and thousands without homes across the region. At this point I decided to sit tight until conditions improved and the clean-up was under way. The border crossing at La Hachadura was closed when I got there on June 1, as the river had washed away the bridge on the Guatemalan side. It was a four-hour ride north to the next border (always supposing the roads were clear), or two back to Juayua. These really weren't conditions in which to take risks so I rode back to the familiar backpacker hostel at Juayua. This was the first time that weather conditions had got the better of me, and my 100-mile (160km) round trip took total mileage to 34,408 (55,374km) just before entering Guatemala.

Juayua
Red Devils – Thai-style tuk-tuks in El Salvador?

Guatemala

Dates in country	Wed 2-Thur 3 June
Number of days	2
Population (millions)	12.5
Capital	Guatemala City
Area (km sq)	109,000
Currency	Quetzal
Entry/exit points	From El Salvador at Ahuachapan. Exit into Mexico at La Mesilla
Total distance miles (km)/date	34,757 (55,936)/Thur 3 June
Average miles (km) per day	105 (169)
Accommodation	Hotel
Food	Another world class coffee-maker
Value	Good
Rating (out of 10)	8

In a nutshell
Stunning scenery; traditional clothing worn in villages; a decent capital city and fledgling tourism industry – but look out for natural disasters.

Route
Guatemala City, Antigua, Huehuetenango.

Rider notes
Bike – All good: the Ténéré is so reliable and maintenance-friendly.

Maps – Freytag & Berndt: *Belize & Guatemala*.

Rider log
I crossed into Guatemala on Wednesday 2 June at Las Chinama: a low-key crossing with the exception of the omnipresent cambio chaps – a greeting party of guys at every border making a small percentage through currency exchange. It's a bit of a game, in a way, and can be a positive experience if the guys are able to make a decent cut on each transaction (and they aim to

Guatemala

Border crossing
What's the best exchange rate for Guatemalan quetzales, please?

Antigua
Welcome to Guatemala

Antigua
Bustling colonial city with lots of useful little shops and fab cafés

Antigua to San Cristobal
I would have liked to potter about the villages a little more, but the storms had caused such devastation, resulting in local frustration at the lack of governmental action that it seemed sensible to keep moving. The bike was looking good – bananas, sandals and water (wedged above exhausts) all sitting happily within the main luggage. Landslides were plentiful on the main highway to Mexico

Guatemala

complete as many as possible). Have an idea of what the exchange rates are, and what you might expect to receive, but don't haggle too hard: equally, of course, try not to get ripped off! Leaving El Salvador and entering Guatemala was both quick and efficient, with photos, paperwork, and even a road tax disc to stick on the inside of the fairing, followed by a short ride of 130 miles (200km) to Antigua. The only way through Guatemala was via its capital due to the previous three days' heavy rain. After Bogota I had promised myself no more big cities but I had no option other than to go through Guatemala City as other routes had been rendered unusable by landslide or flooding.

The city roads were also hazardous but not for this reason: the Volcán de Pacaya had erupted and spewed ash into the city, covering roads, blocking rain ditches and claiming a number of lives, and volcanic ash had been piled up at the end of each road in an attempt to clear them – what next? I wondered – yes, you've guessed it, reports of huge sinkholes appearing, and a massive one in the city. I took it steady and managed to get to a central backpacker hostel that evening, avoiding all the sinkholes, volcanic ash, landslides, flooding, mud on the roads, and usual mopeds, cars, buses and wagons en route.

I had heard exaggerated reports about Guatemala from other travellers concerning roadside bandits and muggings, but, touch wood, I had no problem apart from an aggressive beggar in Antigua, which is very pretty and possibly over-touristy, although this does offer the benefit of good food and a wider choice, albeit at a higher price. The sat nav had begun to play up – the rain, humidity and general daily battering having taken their toll – but it still produced a decent map of my location, which was useful as I'd given up trying to fix it.

The next day's ride to Huehuetenango took in some wonderful farming valleys, though many areas were suffering from the aftermath of tropical Storm Agatha. The infrastructure is just not there to cope with such extreme weather conditions. Parts of the dual carriageway were reduced to single lanes due to mudslides, the collapsed roads necessitating diversions. And this was the main and now only route to Mexico as all of the other roads were closed. Crumpled houses, tin and wooden shacks poked through what looked like an above-water sea bed after mudslides enveloped villages at the side of the road. As in Honduras, people in and around the mud salvaged their belongings where they could. The devastation was a stark contrast to what I'd anticipated seeing – mountain villages with locals in traditional dress – and their faces – tormented, confused and shattered by the recent events caused by the weather – told a sad story. Some looked as if they hadn't slept for a week, which was probably the case. The last ten dangerous and distressing days of the tropical cyclone eventually led to a state of emergency being declared in Guatemala, El Salvador, and Honduras.

Mexico

Dates in country	Fri 4-Mon 21 June
Number of days	18
Population (millions)	110
Capital	Mexico City
Area (km sq)	1,970,000
Currency	Peso
Entry/exit points	From Guatemala at La Democracia. Exit into America at Tecate
Total distance miles (km)/date	37,197 (59,862/Fri 18 June
Average miles (km) per day	190 (306)
Accommodation	Hotel
Food	Tacos – with any filling – including goat head; fresh fruit drinks
Value	Cheap accommodation
Rating (out of 10)	8: Baja California scenery stunning – much nicer than mainland Mexico

In a nutshell
There were lots of military checkpoints along this road, but manned by really friendly guys who just wanted to chat about the bike and what route I'd taken. The World Cup was a good icebreaker.

Route
From La Democracia headed inland to San Cristóbal de la Casas, Palenque, Tuxtla Gutiérrez, Puerto Arista (south of Tonalá), and followed the coast: Mazunte, San Marcos, Zihuantanejo, Barra de Navidad, Los Ayala, Mazatlan – Baja California – La Paz, Loreto, Santa Rosalia, Bahia de los Ángeles, San Vicente.

Rider notes
Bike – Look out for topes (hidden speed humps that are quite severe). Chain replaced at Tuxtla Gutiérrez; oil change at San Marcos.

Mexico

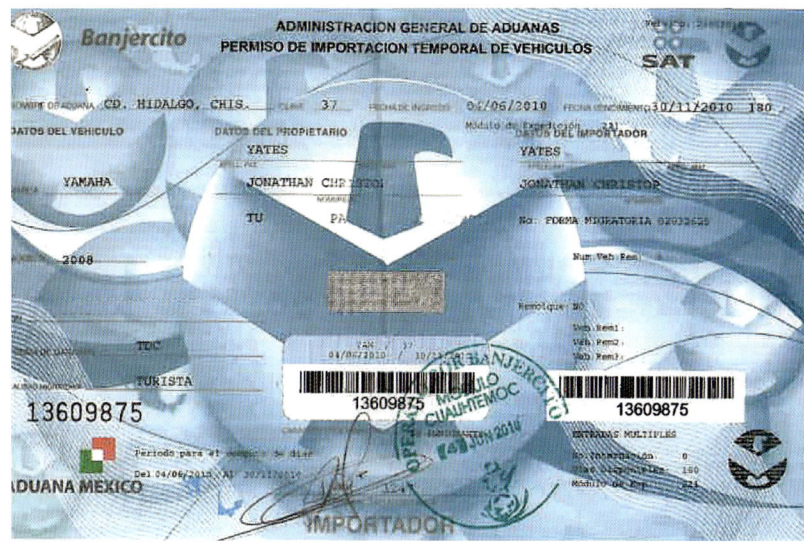

Welcome to Mexico

Mazunte to San Marcos

Danger: tope! Look out for the frustrating and aggressive speed humps, which often appear without warning. I hit one at speed, which gave me quite a shock, though it could have been worse (heading for the back of a bus that has slowed right down over one, which happened on numerous occasions). Locals make their own warning signs

Maps – *International Travel Maps (Mexico)*: excellent map – would recommend this publisher.

Rider log

The ride from Huehuetenango to San Cristóbal (Mexico) was stunning: dropping down from the mountains of Guatemala through numerous

San Cristóbal de las Casas to Palanque
Conditions are hot and dry: always carry extra 'fuel' (bananas and water)

Palanque
Mayan ruins of Palanque and Yaxchilan contrast sharply ...

... with modern activities in the town

traditional villages, I saw local women washing clothes in streams: a very quaint scene but hard work, I'm sure. At the border both Immigration and Customs were quick and efficient – professional. San Cristóbal is the base from which to visit the Palenque Mayan ruins, which was a six-hour ride (I did ask locals how long it might take and got answers ranging from three to eight hours!). Yaxchilan and Bonampak ruins – situated in a remote jungle setting – are also worth a visit.

Halfway to Puerto Arista the next day, a loud grinding noise followed by a clunk and a loss or power told me the bike's chain had broken and come off the rear sprocket, causing minor damage. It was mid-afternoon, hot, and I was stranded. Although there wasn't much in the way of other traffic, I managed to flag down a really kind bloke, Vincent, who offered to load the

Mexico

Palanque to Tuxtla Gutiérrez
Pit stop. Earlier that morning the chain had snagged on a high kerb. Hooray for Vincent the Good Samaritan

bike in the back of his utility/jeep vehicle and drive me to the next town, which was great. However, as the bike is so cumbersome we needed someone else to help load it into the truck, and luckily another Good Samaritan passing realised this and provided the necessary extra muscle. It would have helped to remove the panniers, but, for some reason, Vincent didn't want to do this. He was driving really quickly and the bike was moving about in the back, so he slowed and dribbled to a stop on a hill to let me check and re-secure the bike. Jumping out of the vehicle, I immediately fell down a rain ditch, disappearing from view. Vincent got out to look for me but, as the jeep had no handbrake, it began to roll back down the hill, Vincent hopping alongside trying to get a foot on the brake pedal as I was climbing out the ditch. Thankfully, he managed to stop the van but it was a real comic moment.

We arrived at Tuxtla Gutiérrez and found a motorbike shop which claimed to do servicing and repairs. I wasn't convinced as the 'showroom' consisted of only a small number of kiddies' Chinese-manufacture quad bikes.

The previous night the owner of the hotel where I'd stayed had allowed me to store the bike in the shop unit under the hotel, and, though riding in was okay, getting the bike out backwards the next morning was more problematic, and we'd caught the underside on a huge kerb. In hindsight, I think the chain had been damaged on the kerbstone, causing it to break later.

I returned to the bike shop the following morning as agreed but there was no mechanic. After playing around with the chain for the best part of an hour, it became obvious that me and the shop owner (who was more sales than workshop) weren't going to fix it. A mechanic from another bike shop appeared and we walked to a Yamaha dealer (my mistake was not making "Yamaha?" my first question when I'd arrived), which had a chain but wouldn't sell it to me. By this time I was becoming agitated. Twenty minutes later the Yamaha mechanic appeared on the street corner with the chain and some spare links, chasing a cash payment, the money for which, strangely, went into his own pocket and not the till (a bonus, perhaps?). We did the deal and I returned to the original bike shop to have the chain fitted, which I would have preferred to have had done at the Yamaha dealership, but there was obviously some bad blood between the dealership and the shop where my bike was, so the Yamaha chaps weren't interested. It was an odd situation and, although accompanied by some amateurish and quite serious whacking, the new chain was eventually on, and I was glad to be on the road again the following morning, Wednesday 9 June.

The Mexicans were really into the World Cup, and football dominated the country. When Mexico was playing the roads were free of traffic, with trucks, cars and even buses parked up at the cafés that had TVs. The World Cup was a great conversation topic with locals, although some places weren't quite as friendly. I rode past a massive rock/boulder on the side of the road which had on it 'Fuck you, Greengo' ('Gringo' incorrectly spelt), and going through the next town I was given the V-sign. This, combined with reports of gangsters, drug cartels and towns/cities on the border with no police presence, kept me on my toes. (After riding through Acapulco I later read reports of a number of headless bodies being found in wheelie bins – Mexico's gangs control many of the big towns and cities.)

Saturday 12 June was pretty much an average day in Mexico. I'd been keeping a really close eye on the new chain; oiling and checking it very early each morning as I headed north to Acapulco, where I planned to overnight. Hitting roadworks just outside the city, I decided instead to motor on, and it took two-and-a-half hours to do 50 miles (80km), including being stopped by a really dodgy transit cop who, in the scorching heat, bumbled on for about

Zihuantanejo to Barra de Navidad
(main and top left)

La Paz to Loreto
(top right)

Bahia de los Angeles to San Vicente
(left)

The road is long: checkpoints; surf, and dusty towns

15 minutes before finally asking if I could do him a favour (translation: give him some money). By this time, I'd really had enough of all these bent cops: none of the military in Mexico ask for money, just the cops, and this guy was particularly irksome, claiming I was carrying lots of cash. I told him "no" and sat down at the roadside. Everyone was looking at me – bus passengers and pedestrians – as it looked as if the cop was giving me a bollocking, when in fact he was asking for cash. Trying a different tactic, the cop then claimed I didn't stop correctly for the roadworks, but he met with the same response from me and, in the end, gave up. I was pleased to have held out, though did worry a bit that he might radio ahead to his colleagues to make things difficult for me at future checkpoints.

Stopping for lunch I discovered new varieties of taco filling: meat from the skulls of goats. Nice. There must have been a BBQ the previous evening as skulls sat amongst a tray of goat meat which was just grim. I'd had tacos with cheese, chicken, chicken and cheese, fish, mixed beef, pork, and now goat. I decided that, if offered Mexican back home, I would have to decline.

The further north into Mexico I travelled, the more like America it became, with Burger King, Subway, and Walmart outlets in most cities. A few rain clouds appeared but they didn't break, which was good, as this gave me my first full dry day since Panama. After a ride of 119 miles (190km) – 36,065 (54,041km) total – I arrived at Zihuantanejo and called it a day.

The ride through the rest of Mexico was uneventful, taking me straight up the coast and a ferry across to Baja California, then continuing north through desert scrubland and stunning coastline bays and marinas.

Unfortunately, I hit problems leaving Mexico at Tecate. I queue-jumped the massed traffic, trickling past some hundred or so cars by squeezing through the narrowest of gaps. Confusion amongst officials on both sides of the border meant I somehow rode from Mexico straight into America, after a female US Immigration Officer checked my passport and waved me through. I dribbled through the checkpoint to be halted at the very last minute by another officer who wanted to check my papers, and accused me of not having the necessary paperwork. The female officer who had waved me through hadn't given me any of the documents I needed: apparently she was a new recruit – whaaat?

It was all a bit confused – which didn't tie in at all with reports I'd heard about how strict the controls between Mexico and USA are. My fingerprints were eventually taken and a visa waiver approved, but the one step I had missed – Customs exit papers on the Mexican side – meant I had to go back into Mexico to get my passport stamped by Customs, as they refused to process the bike at the border, not giving a reason why. The Mexican

Mexico

Given all the reported issues of illegal crossings into America, I'd expected the process to be well organised, when in fact it was a farce.

Leaving the border area at 1.30 that afternoon, I rode 316 miles (500km) into the US to Joshua Tree National Park (total mileage 38,071/61,269km), very glad to be amongst some English-speaking folks again.

Bahia de los Angeles to San Vicente
Baja California was relaxing riding compared to the 'mainland.' However, it was extremely hot and the desert vultures were circling: if I came off would mine be the next sunbleached rack of ribs?

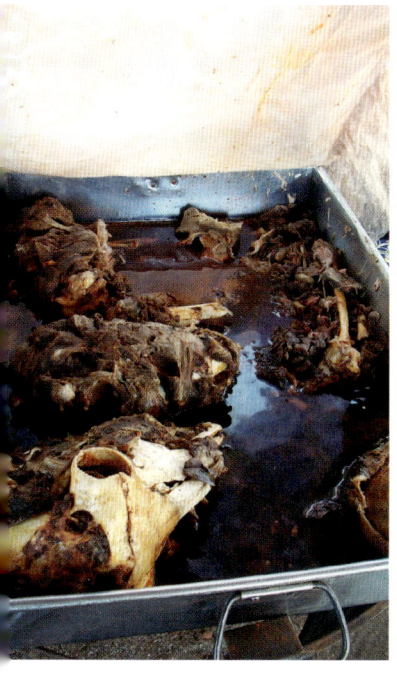

San Marcos to Zihuantanejo
Food and drink. You never know what to expect on the road, but the key principle is simple: if it's busy and the locals are buying it, it's good. Two extremes: 1) amazingly fresh smoothies: by mid-morning this stand was five deep in people; 2) goat head and tacos: "Okay, I'll try one" (followed by a shaky "thanks")

authorities suggested I ride to Tijuana, a couple of hours east, to properly exit Mexico but I simply wasn't prepared to do this – it would involve further cost and paperwork as I would have to exit the US – and I didn't have the energy anyway. In any case, what could they do? The bike was already legally in the US and the entry paperwork was complete.

Walking from the Mexican Customs through border control I pondered my options. Arriving back at the bike, thinking to myself "too much bureaucracy," I started the engine and rode into America: adios, Mexico!

United States of America

Dates in country	Mon 21 June-Sun 11 July
Number of days	20
Population (millions)	300
Capital	Washington DC
Area (km sq)	9,630,000
Currency	US dollar
Entry/exit points	From Mexico at Tecate. Exit into Canada at Waterton-Glacier International Peace Park
Total distance miles (km)/date	41,319 (66,496) /Fri 9 July
Average miles (km) per day	135 (217)
Accommodation	Camping (100%)
Food	Burgers, BBQs, and good breakfasts
Value	Tip – try to share National Park pitches with other small groups to save money, and erect your tent in the shade in Utah
Rating (out of 10)	9

In a nutshell
Amazing National Parks; excellent camping; easy scenic riding – a great way to wind down after a global ride.

Route
Crossed into the USA at Tecate and spent the first few nights at Joshua Tree National Park. Visited some amazing National Parks and points of interest,

Start the day right!

United States of America

including: Lake Havasu; Grand Canyon NP; Vermilion Cliffs; Zion NP; Bryce; Capitol Reef; Arches NP; Grand Teeton NP; Yellowstone NP; Glacier/Waterton National Parks. And I didn't travel on a single highway!

Rider notes
Look out for pensioners on Harleys!
Bike – Replacement chain after Mexican repair failed (not surprisingly).
Maps – *Rand McNally Road Atlas: US, Canada, Mexico.*

Rider log
It was a relief to leave Mexico and ride into America at the small border crossing of Tecate, which is wedged in-between its two bigger border crossing neighbours, Tijuana and Mexicali. I chose to cross at Tecate following lots of advice to do so from American trippers on the Baja, although, unfortunately, it wasn't simple. I called and emailed the Mexican SAT (Secretaria de Administratión y Tributaria), which oversees goods in and out of Mexico, later that week, but to this day don't know whether or not my bike is still registered in Mexico following the border crossing debacle.

From the border it was a hot, dry ride to the outstanding Joshua Tree National Park where I camped for two days. This was the first of about fifteen National, State and Recreation Parks dotted around up to the Canadian border.

The first problem I encountered was what I call the pizza dilemma. In contrast to most of the countries I rode through, in the US it works out cheaper to buy the big size ('Go Large!') than the small. For example, an 8 inch pizza with one topping cost $8 (£5), but a 14 inch pizza with every topping I wanted was only $10 (£6), so I had to go for the larger one as who wants a pizza with just one topping? And the stereotyping about Americans is true, I'm afraid: I saw lots of pretty hefty citizens. 'Go Large' promotions equal a 'Go Large' population; I couldn't help but compare this to the free recreational exercise equipment I frequently saw being used in most Chinese towns and city parks.

Fuelling in California was a nightmare, though, due to very sensitive sensors in the gas nozzles which pick up on fuel vapour. As the tank on a bike is smaller, the sensor causes the pump to cut out straight away, preventing you from filling up. It's a complete shambles, really, as you also have to pre-pay for fuel. I'd just about mastered this system the morning I left for Arizona, where the process is different.

As I'd expected, roads were good with the exception of a few weird junctions in city centres (crossroads and stop signs in the grid system). Saw lots of bikes – always Harley Davidsons – whose riders were happy to chat. It was a relief to be back in an English-speaking country.

On Thursday 24 June the replacement chain that had been rather inexpertly fitted in Mexico gave way whilst I was trundling along at 55mph (88kph), heading east to the Grand Canyon. Hearing clunking noises, I knew immediately what was causing it: a pin had come out of a section of chain. Riding very slowly to the next junction, I discoverd to my amazement that

Joshua Tree National Park
First stop in the US. Take time out, set up camp, and enjoy the natural beauty of the park

Grand Canyon to Coral Pink Sand Dunes State Park

route to the Canyon through Sedona, Flagstaff and Kaibab National Forest was fabulous. Total mileage at the Grand Canyon: 38,825 (62,482km).

I took Route 89 from the Grand Canyon, which stretches into Utah up to Zion National Park via Coral Pink Sand Dunes State Park. Utah was just incredible, and home to amazing National Parks such as Capitol Reef, Canyons of the Escalante, and Arches (total mileage 40,301/64,858km).

By Monday 6 July I had arrived at Yellowstone National Park (mileage 41,225/66,345km), where I enjoyed free camping in a small state park between Yellowstone and Grand Teeton National Park. I found a really sweet spot right by a river, from where I saw massive moose and even a bear on the morning I decamped. It was simply fantastic. Yellowstone leads naturally to Glacier National Park via a really quiet road – the 83 – which meanders through three or four national forests, and past the really big Flathead Lake. I camped at Lost Johnny Campground alongside Hungry Horse Reservoir that evening.

After 244 miles (392km) of great riding through America's spectacular scenery – during which I saw mountain goats, great lakes, and lots of deer – my mileage just south of Canada totalled 41,991 (67,577km).

Don't bother with Route 66: the 83 is a real classic!

just half a mile away was a Harley Davidson garage that also sold Yamahas. I tapped the pin back in and nursed the bike to the garage, and the helpful staff fitted a new chain almost immediately, allowing me to jump the queue ahead of their scheduled workload. Because of the pit stop I fell short of Grand Canyon and stayed at a place called Dead Horse Ranch campground outside Cottonwood.

Arizona's biggest claim to fame is the Grand Canyon, and even the

United States of America

Utah Classics
The scenery through Utah and its National Parks was simply stunning: who needs Route 66?; south to north beats east to west hands down

THE REAL WAY ROUND

Arches National Park to High Lake State Park On-the-road conditions were perfect for riding: I had a couple of runs at this sweeping bend, and even on the Ténéré was able to get my knee down

Arches National Park

Camping, riding and generally tramping about the US National Parks was a relaxing and economical way to end the trip

Yellowstone National Park

(right & overleaf) 'Beware of the Dog' just doesn't cover it in Yellowstone. Why did the Bison cross the road? Camping with bears? Although incredibly popular, it was still possible to find quiet places within the park; the hot springs and Old Faithful geyser are two of the main attractions

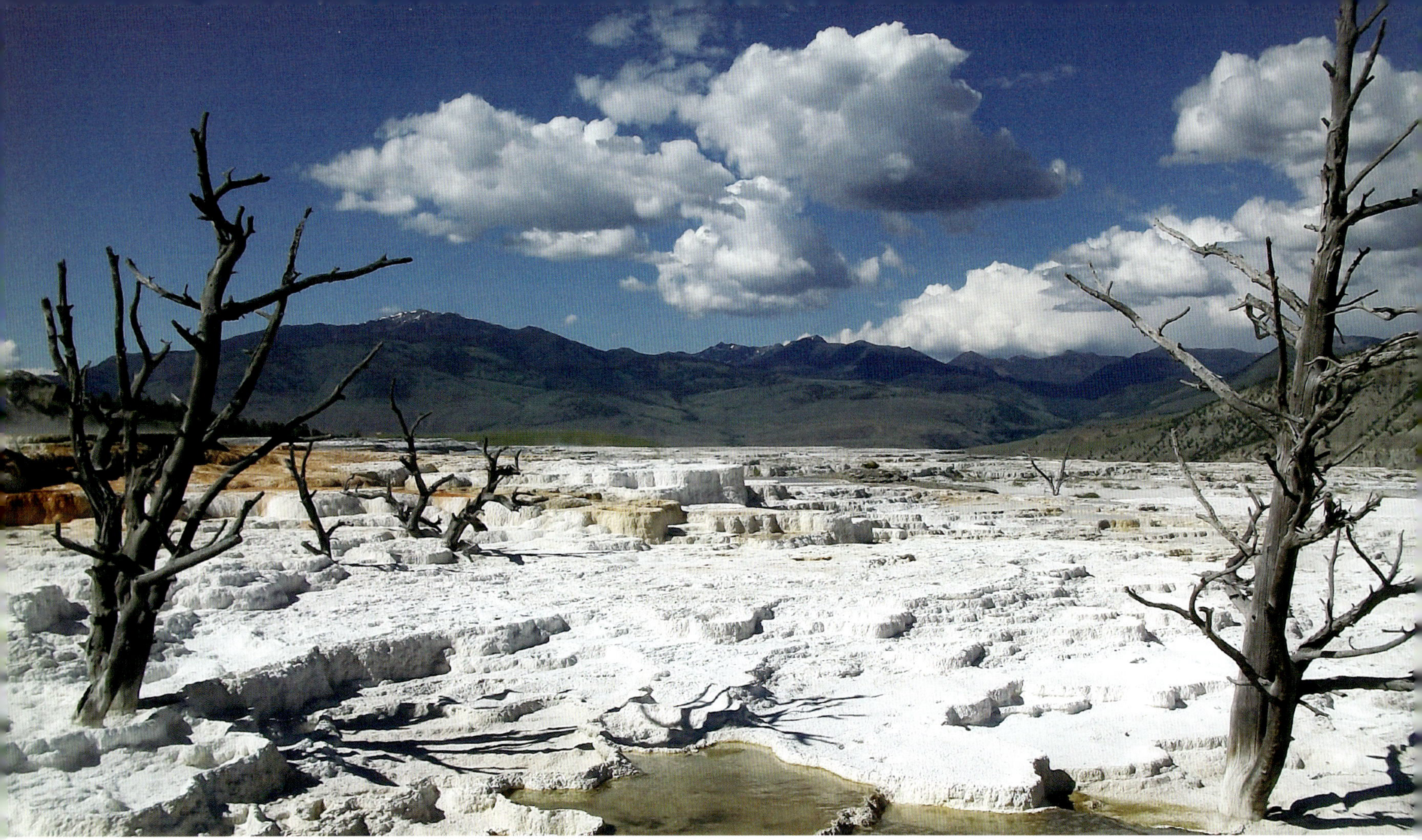

WARNING
06/14/2010
BEAR
FREQUENTING AREA
Removal of this sign may result in INJURY to others
and is punishable by law

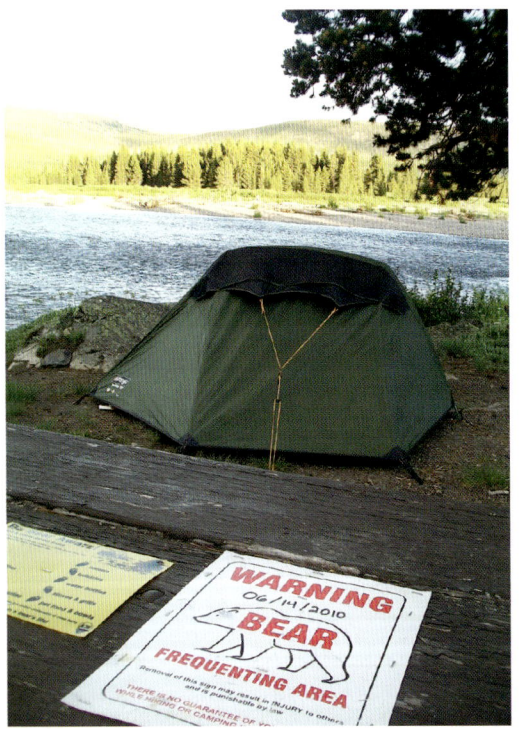

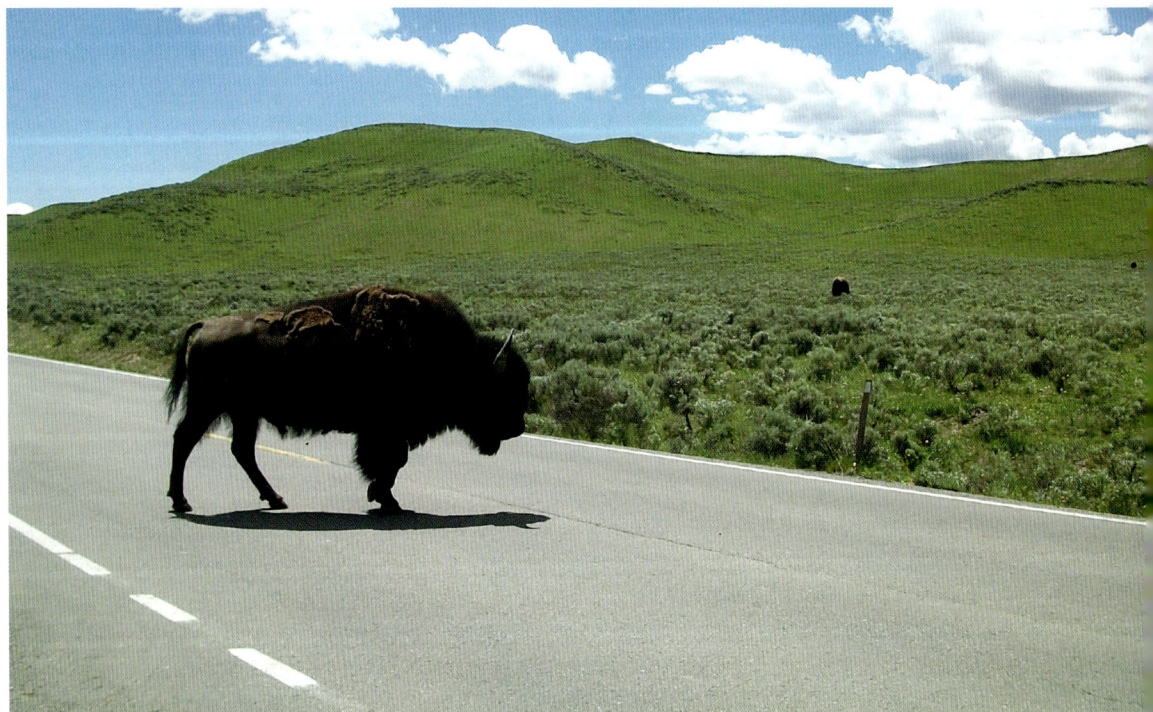

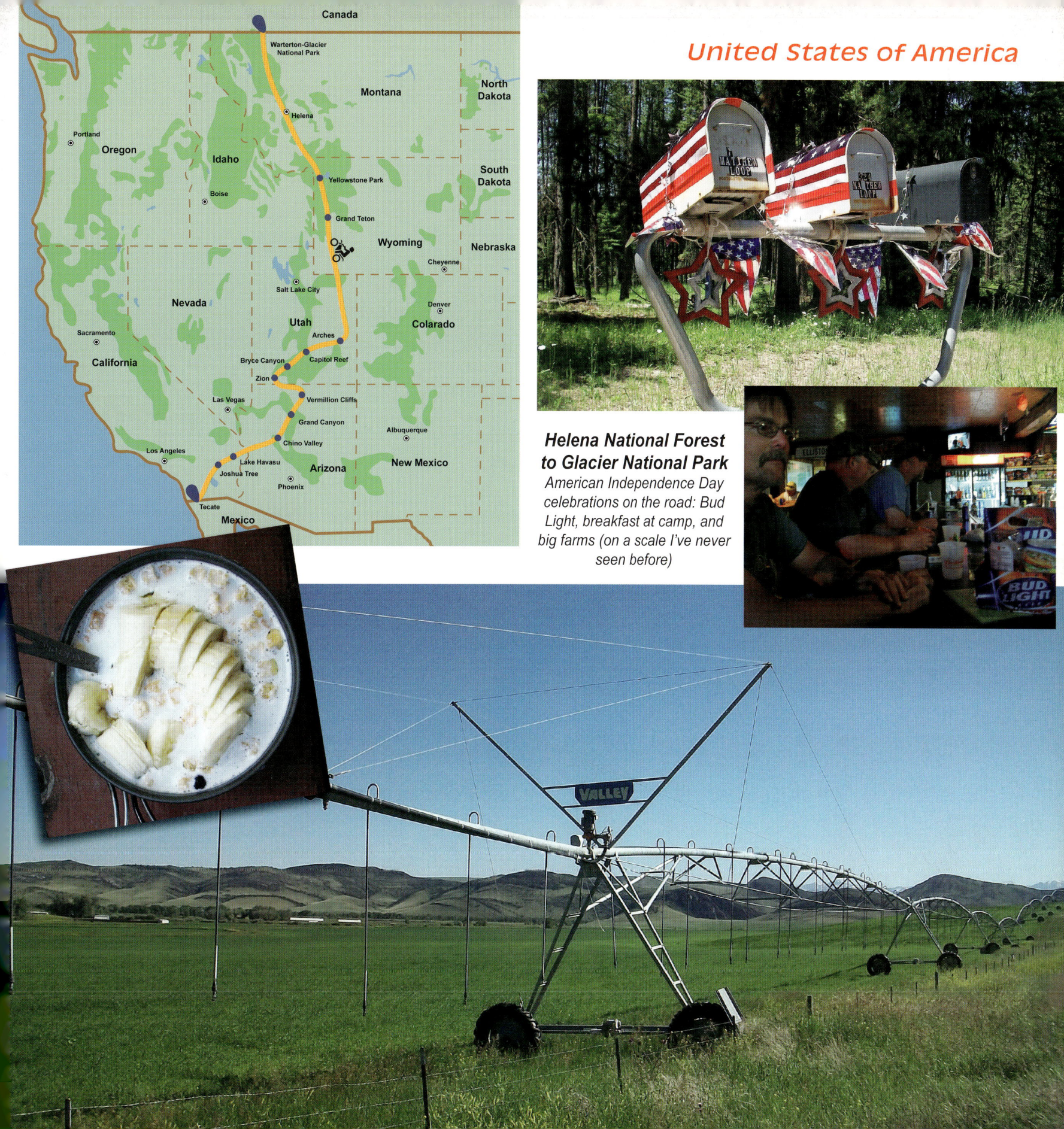

United States of America

Helena National Forest to Glacier National Park
American Independence Day celebrations on the road: Bud Light, breakfast at camp, and big farms (on a scale I've never seen before)

Yellowstone and Glacier National Parks

Canada

Dates in country	*Mon 12-Wed 21 July*
Number of days	*10*
Population (millions)	*33*
Capital	*Ottawa*
Area (km sq)	*9,984,000*
Currency	*Canadian dollar*
Entry/exit points	*From America at Glacier/Waterton National Park. Exit from Calgary to London, England*
Total distance miles (km)/date	*41,642 (67,016)/Fri 16 July*
Average miles (km) per day	*130 (209) (rode for two days only)*
Accommodation	*Camping/friend's house and Lakeside Lodge*
Food	*Great, especially in Calgary Tower (observation tower) where I had steak and Canadian red wine*
Value	*Same as UK (expensive)*
Rating (out of 10)	*8*

In a nutshell
Calgary Stampede (annual rodeo, exhibition and festival): the Canadians know how to party!

Route
Pincher Creek, Turner Valley, Calgary, Red Deer, Lacombe; back to Calgary.

Rider notes
Didn't do much riding but I'm sure it would be excellent if the limited mileage I did is anything to go by. Would like to return and do more, one day.
Bike – Time to pack it up and send it back to the UK.
Maps – *Rand McNally Road Atlas: US, Canada, Mexico*.

Rider log
On Saturday 11 July I made the short ride through Glacier National Park that takes road trippers into Canada and Waterton National Park, with a total mileage of 42,083 (67,726km) on entering the final country of my trip

Canada

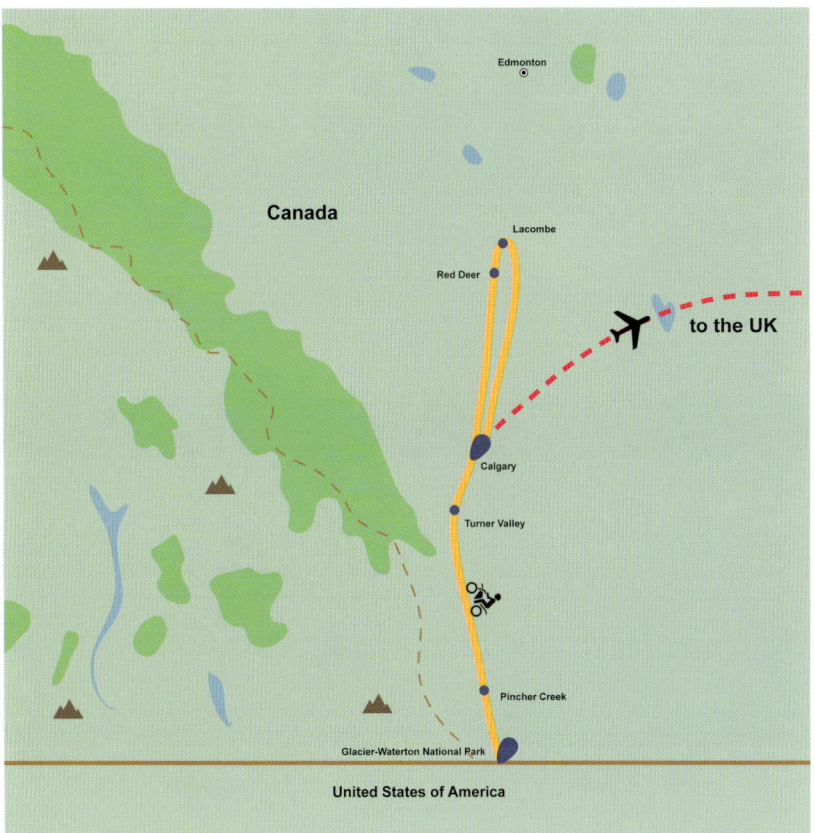

Glacier and Waterton National Parks to Calgary
The road to Calgary: a two-day home straight after my year-long ride ...
... rather unconventional hat stands – more than 3 miles of 'em

(in ten days' time I would be at Calgary airport to organise freight to the UK for the bike). This must be the most scenic border crossing ever, wedged, as it is, between two National Parks, only slightly marred by an over-zealous Immigration Officer who seemed so full of his own importance that he was unable to even make conversation. Handing back my stamped American visa waiver, he briefly checked the bike and enquired about my destination. I was in Canada.

The weather was good at the crossing but a storm was imminent, so I called it a day at the first town – Pincher Creek – after riding for a while through endlessly-scenic landscapes. On arrival I refuelled and withdrew money from an ATM: Canadian dollars featuring the Queen – wow! I was close to home now and the end of my journey. Pincher Creek was a small town of about 5000 people, with not much to do so I went for a relaxing swim in the local pool to avoid the wet weather and wind that had arrived.

At my final destination of Calgary – a fabulous city – my trip was complete on Monday 13 July with a total of 42,371 miles (68,189km). I met up with a number of friends who I had originally got to know during the Antarctic expedition, and together we explored the city and experienced the Stampede, a ten-day event that bills itself as 'The Greatest Outdoor Show on Earth.' Attracting over a million visitors, it can only be described as the world's biggest rodeo: featuring shows of horsemanship, a parade, midway, stage shows, concerts, agricultural competitions, chuckwagon racing and First Nations exhibitions. Following this I spent a weekend north of Calgary at Gull Lake (halfway to Edmonton), which is a popular recreational lake with southern shores that boast large, sandy beaches.

The 16-mile (25km) ride to the airport (total 42,387/68,215km) felt odd: such a short stint to end the longest of trips. Insignificant in terms of mileage and experience, but momentous nonetheless, as it was the last time I would complete my daily routine of the last year: donning boots, jacket, helmet; mounting the sat nav in its bracket; turning on the ignition and thumbing the starter button. I was ready to return to the UK, happy at the thought of seeing friends and family once again, but could just have easily carried on toward Alaska, revelling in the freedom of riding solo, exploring and meeting new people along the way. Mixed emotions, indeed ...

On July 21 I boarded a flight to Gatwick. During the flight home I struggled to relax, looking through some of the photos from my trip, remembering all the things I'd seen and experienced. Had I really ridden round the world? What an amazing journey of a lifetime ...

Calgary
Calling all Cowboys! The Calgary Stampede: what a show, and what a finale to my trip!

Calgary
In the city. Stampede fever touches parts other festivals cannot. Spray tan: really? Calgary tower and the view from it

Epilogue

One of the interesting aspects about riding through different countries is experiencing how the same task is managed (or not), and this can range from simple things such as booking into a campsite or refuelling, to more complex exercises such as shipping the bike.

For example, refuelling in China had to be done by filling kettles with fuel and taking these to the bike, which was not allowed into the petrol station for fear that the exposed engine might ignite, whilst refuelling direct from the tanker was acceptable in Kazakhstan! More complicated tasks – such as exit formalities for the bike at Customs – varied even more. Leaving Indonesia, the entire process was completed by just one individual who checked documents and stamped the Carnet de Passage, compared to Australia where a pre-booked appointment was required, and two inspectors plus three other officials had to stamp and authorise the paperwork.

When I look back and think of all the places I have been, I can hardly believe I have experienced so much. I have seen some fabulous sights; met some great people, and visited remote villages: for example, those in East Timor with a population of just 20 people, as well as busy cities like Sydney and Buenos Aires. The contrast between countries in close proximity such as Australia and Timor, and Italy and Bosnia can be mind-blowing, as it's like going back a hundred years when really they are only hours apart. Seeing people in villages in China and Indonesia having to farm the land so hard made a hobby allotment in America seem like a luxury: doing the same sort of thing for pleasure rather than because lives depended upon it.

Within countries differences are marked: Kazakhstani cities are developed and home to BMWs and Mercedes, but in the desert – and elsewhere, such as certain cities and villages in China – people had very little: there are so very many contrasts. (One constant in Kazakhstan, however, was that the people were very friendly, whether in city or village, and it's this that shaped the trip for me.)

The difference in attitude toward motorcycles in various countries is worth noting. In China, for example, it's bad, and bikes are actually banned from certain cities, the highway and petrol stations. Malaysia, in contrast, has a fantastic attitude, and bikes are exempt from toll charges, have a separate express lane to access the highway, and there are regular shelters in case of a rainstorm.

It's important to keep moving at a sensible pace: I could have stayed longer in many countries but at the cost of another experience in a different country. Travel at a speed that you find enjoyable – it's not a race. I rode for approximately 250 days of the year, so a third of the time I was off the bike.

A few basics. Avoid overnighting at border towns (there are better places to stay), and don't become frustrated by repeated irritations such as border crossings, where it can sometimes seem that the same jobsworth is asking you the same questions at every crossing. Eat fresh fruit and, where possible, choose the busiest cafes to eat lunch in.

Don't overpack – local markets tend to have everything – and people in emerging countries are incredibly resourceful, able to fix anything, it seems.

Gatwick to Preston, England
Welcome home with some great British classics: steak and kidney pie with HP sauce, fish and chips with mushy peas, and – of course – speed cameras

My kit, unpacked

Once outside of the UK (perhaps Europe) I was amazed at the 'repair it, don't throw it away' culture, and there are too many examples to list. Keep things simple and don't over-spec with gadgets or over-modify the bike, as there's just no need.

If something causes a delay, enjoy it! You're not on a schedule so take advantage of the hold-up and have a break: after all, you'll need some time off, so make the most of an opportunity to relax for a while.

Choose the right bike to do the trip on. I haven't said a lot about this and don't feel I need to; for me, the Yamaha Ténéré is the one. When I left the UK I had ridden fewer than 10,000 miles (16,000km) on the Fazer and running-in the Ténéré combined. On my return to the UK, service and repairs came to just £407.66, which included general wear and tear, rear damper, bearings, nuts and sprocket. The bike is a real credit to Yamaha.

The *Revelation* article I grabbed from the Tasmanian backpacker hostel espoused: 'Work on your head and your heart or you'll be the same person when you return at the end of the journey.' Well, I am the same person, still, but I've experienced situations, events, cultures and challenges that have undoubtedly made me more open-minded and tolerant of differences, and able to put into perspective my daily events, both on and off the bike. A journey such as this stretches the scale of experience to the limits, and tests ability to the extreme. It can be tough, and I think a certain degree of determination is needed on most days to deal with challenging conditions (such as a gusty ride in Patagonian gale force winds) and people (antagonistic Ukrainian police).

Get yourself a bike and get planning, then ride to the nearest border. I can honestly say that a biker in a foreign land is generally met with a warm reception. To really experience different cultures as they actually are, meet the locals and visit hidden-away places (as well as the famous ones). Keep an open mind, and be willing to take a few calculated risks: don't believe all that the doom-mongers say (including Lonely Planet's 'Dangers and Annoyances' section) as, rather than muggings and bandits, chances are you'll be met with friendliness and warmth.

Keep smiling, get out of your comfort zone (every day), shake hands with strangers, make considered decisions after talking to locals – and set off soon as the world is changing. Enjoy!

Index

Aguachica 167
Air freight 5, 8
Aktobe 32
Alice Springs 110, 116, 120
Antarctica 3, 122, 123, 133, 135, 137, 142, 215
Antigua 194-197
AQIS form 112
Arches National Park 206
Arenal Volcano 179-181
Argentina 3, 6, 8, 23, 113, 122, 123, 126, 128, 130, 132, 133, 137, 139, 141, 142, 147, 149, 151, 153
Arica 149, 151-153, 155
Arnay-le-Duc 11
Astrakhan 27-29, 32, 36-38
Atlantic 122, 132
Australia 3, 4, 6, 73, 79, 92, 106, 107, 109-113, 115, 116, 118, 122, 132, 218
Ayres Rock (Uluru) 117, 118

Bahia de los Ángeles 198
Bahia de Salinas 179, 180
Bahia Salinas 183, 184
Baja California 198, 202, 203
Bajawa 89, 97-100, 103
Bali 85, 91, 92, 96, 104
Bandung 88, 89, 103
Bang Saphan 70, 71, 73, 75, 76
Bangkok 65, 66, 70-75
Banking 5
Baoding 63, 64
Baoji 61
Bariloche 123, 133, 137, 149
Barra de Navidad 198, 202
Batugade 83, 100-102, 106-108
Baturaja 85, 87, 95
Beijing 12, 14, 50, 53, 65, 66, 69, 70
Belawan Port 81, 84, 89
Belén 123
Bicaz 21, 22
Bihac 16-18
Bike kit 7
Bike modifications 6, 95
Bike skills and knowledge 6
Bike test 4

Bishkek 39, 41, 45, 46
Black Sea 27, 28
Bogota 167, 173, 175, 176, 197
Bolivia 3, 122, 142, 143, 145, 146
Bosnia and Herzegovina 16-18
Brașov 20, 24
Budget 5, 8, 12, 49, 86, 110, 126, 137, 153
Buenos Aires 5, 119, 121-124, 126-128, 131, 218
Bukittinggi 85, 95
Butterworth 78, 81

Cadney Homestead 115, 119
Calama 149
Calgary 165, 214-216
Camana 153, 155, 156, 158
Camera 6, 119
Cameron Highlands 78-81, 85
Canada 3, 8, 204-206, 214, 215, 217
Cartagena 159, 167, 171, 172, 174
Casma 153, 157-159
Chamonix-Mont-Blanc 11
Charyn Gorge 32, 49
Chiclayo 153, 156, 158-161, 163
Chilca 153, 157
Chile 3, 6, 113, 122, 126, 133, 137, 138, 147, 149, 151, 153, 160
Chilli 32
China 3, 5, 6, 8, 12, 28, 30, 32, 38, 39, 42, 43, 45, 49-51, 53-55, 57, 59, 60, 66, 67, 71, 73, 85, 156, 157, 218
Cholpon-Ata 39
Choluteca 182, 186
Cluses 11
Colombia 3, 160, 167-171, 173, 176
Communications and technology 5
Coober Pedy 115, 118, 119
Coral Pink Sand Dunes State Park 206
Costa Rica 3, 176-179, 182, 185
Croatia 3, 10, 11, 13-19
Cuenca 160-165
Cuenca Canton 161-165
Customs 7, 8, 27, 29, 49, 53, 54, 66, 73, 82, 107, 110-113, 121, 161, 168, 173, 175, 177, 185, 192, 200, 202, 203, 218

Darwin 73, 79, 101, 106, 109-113, 115, 116
David 176
Dengfeng 60, 62
Devils Marbles 115, 117
Dili 73, 101, 106-110
Dolon pass 39
Dominical 178-180
Dunhuang 63, 64

Eastern Euope 16
Ecuador 3, 153, 160, 161, 165-167
El Calafate 130, 131, 133, 137
El Salvador 3, 182, 186, 189-191, 193, 194, 197
England 3, 10, 11, 69, 112, 115, 116, 159, 168, 177, 214, 219
Esperanza 130, 133, 137
Europe 3, 5, 7, 8, 10-13, 16, 23, 28, 32, 219, 222
Euros 10, 12, 15

Fish and chips 110, 219
Flinders Ranges 115-117, 119, 120
Flores 85, 89, 98, 101, 104
Flores Kelimutu National Park 98
France 3, 10-13

Gatwick 73, 215, 219
General Alvear, 123
Glacier and Waterton National Parks 206, 214, 215
Gospić 11
Granada 182-185
Grand Canyon 205, 206
Great Wall 60
Guadalupe 176, 177, 180
Guatemala 3, 189, 193-195, 197-199
Gulja 50, 51, 54-56, 59, 60, 67

Hat Chong Ke 70, 73, 77
Hat Tham Phra Nang National Park 70
Hat Yai 70
Helena National Forest 211
Home administration 8
Honduras 3, 182, 186, 187, 189, 197
Horizons Unlimited 5
HP sauce 219
Huanchaco 159
Huehuetenango 194, 197, 199
Hungary 3, 16, 17, 19, 20
Hunter Valley 115, 119, 121

Ibarra 160, 166, 168, 169

Indonesia 3-5, 8, 73, 78, 80-85, 89, 91, 92, 97, 101, 106, 108, 113, 116, 132, 139, 158, 167-169, 218
Insurance 5, 8, 29, 126, 185
Ipoh 78
Irgiz 32-35
Italy 3, 10-14, 17, 218

Java 85, 88, 90, 93, 104
JD Wetherspoon 5
Jiayuguan 60
Joshua Tree National Park 203-205
Juayua 189-193
Jupiter's Travels 5

Karaköl-Charyn Canyon 45, 49
Karkara 30, 32
Katherine 113-115
Kazakhstan 3, 5, 9, 29-34, 37, 38, 45, 49, 50, 54, 73, 75, 113, 116, 218
Kedah 78
Kedisan 92
Kefamenanu 100-103
Keng-Suu 39
Khao Sok National Park 70
Khmelnytskyi 27, 28
Kit 5-9, 12, 27, 71, 82, 85, 91, 98, 106, 116, 133, 164, 189, 219
Kochkor 39-41, 47, 48
Koktal Zharkent 32
Korday 30-32, 37-39
Korgas 30, 32, 53
Krabbi (Ao Nang) 70
Krasnyy Yar 25, 30, 32
Kumul 53, 64
Kupang 100-104
Kutoajaro 89-91, 103
Kuytun 57
Kyrgyzstan 32, 39
Kyzlorda 32
Kyzylorda 35

Labuan 104
Lacombe 214
La Democracia 198
Laem Son National Park 70, 71, 75, 76
Lake Como 11
Lake Garda 11
Lake Geneva 11, 12
Lake Issyk Kol 39-41
Lake Maggoire 11
Lake Saint Claire 115, 119
Language 5, 12, 82, 124, 130, 178
Lanzhou 61, 66

La Paz 198, 202
La Pintada 167-169, 172, 173
Larantuka 98, 101, 104
Las Grutas 129
León 182, 184-187
Lignano Sabbiadoro 11, 13
Linghao 62
Lombok 85, 92, 93, 96, 104
Lonely Planet 70, 98, 186, 219
Loreto 198, 202
Los Ayala 198
Lovina beach 99
Lubahanbajo 89, 97, 103
Lubuklinggau 84, 85, 87, 95, 102, 103
Lugovoy 31, 32
Lújan De Cuyo 123

Macara 153, 156, 158-163
Makat 32, 36-38
Makó 16, 19
Malyasia 70
Mariupol' 26-28
Mataram 96, 104
Mazatlan 198
Mazunte 198, 199
Melbourne 107, 111-113
Mexico 3, 8, 193, 194, 196-199, 201-205, 214
Mildura 116
Mondo Enduro 5
Moni 98
Moquegua 153, 155, 156
MotoExplorers 28, 39, 42, 43
Muara Bungo 84, 85, 87, 95, 102, 103
Mugger's wallet 5
Munduk 89, 91, 92
Museum of the Revolution 185, 193

Nacaome 182
Naryn 39, 41-43, 45, 46
Nazca 153, 155-158
Nicaragu 182
Nicaragua 3, 179, 180, 182, 183, 185, 186
Novokazalinsk 32, 35
Nyon 11

Odesa 25-28
Oktyabrsk 32
Orašje 17
Orto-Tokoy 39, 41
Osp 11-14
Overlanders checklist 7

Padang Sidempuan 85, 87-89
Palanque 200, 201
Panama 3, 167, 171, 173, 176, 177, 179, 202
Paperwork 8, 9, 27, 39, 49, 53, 54, 73, 82, 84, 107, 113, 121, 126, 156, 161, 168, 173, 175, 177, 197, 202, 203, 218
Parit Buntar 79
Pasto 167-169, 171, 172, 174
Patagonia 131, 133, 137, 149
Pedro Luro 129
Penang 78, 81, 82
Penisula Valdes 123
Perquin 189-193
Peru 3, 126, 142, 149, 153, 156, 157, 159, 160, 166, 184
Phattalung 70
Photos 6, 23, 32, 34, 66, 77, 82, 86, 87, 166, 170, 197, 215
Pincher Creek 214, 215
Piura 153, 159, 160
Planning whilst riding 8
Plitvička Jezera 10, 11, 13-15, 17
Popayán 167, 168, 171, 172, 174
Port Augusta 110, 113, 119
Prent 11
Preston 10, 11, 219
Puerto Arista 198, 200
Puerto Madryn 123
Puerto Montt 123, 133, 137, 139, 149
Puerto Natales 123, 137, 149
Puerto Pirámides 129
Puerto San Julian 123, 129
Punta Arenas 149

RAC Carnet de Passage En Douane 7
Rada Tilly (Comodoro Rivadavia) 123, 129
Rădăuți 20
Red Centre 113, 116, 118, 122, 141
Red Deer 214
Refuelling 23, 37, 67, 96, 122, 218
Renmark 115, 116, 120
Renner Springs 112, 114, 115
Revelation 4, 5, 219
Ribakovka 26, 27
Rijeka 11
Riobamba 160, 165
Rio Gallegos 123
Rio Grande 123, 130, 133, 137
Rio Hato 176-178
Rivas 102
Romania 3, 16, 17, 19, 20, 23, 28, 77

Rostov-on-Don 26, 28
Route planning 6, 15, 79, 82
Russia 3, 5, 8, 14, 25, 27-30, 32, 34, 54, 73

Salta 122-124, 139, 141, 142, 144, 147, 149
Sambatta 20
Samosir Island 85, 86, 88, 89
San Carlos de Bariloche 123
San Cristóbal de la Casas 196, 198
San Gil 167
San Jose 179, 180
San Juan 123, 141, 143
San Marcos 198, 199, 203
San Miguel 139, 141, 143, 189
San Salvador 189
San Vicente 189, 198, 202, 203
Santa Ana 189
Santa Clara 189, 190
Santa Rosalia 198
Sape 93, 98, 104
Seminyak beach 99
Serbia 3, 16, 17, 19
Shijiazhuang 63-65
Shubarkuduk 33, 34
Shymkent 30, 32, 34
Simplon Pass 11, 13
Škocjanske jame 11, 13
Slovenia 3, 10-14
Solo 4, 5, 12, 14, 88, 90, 91, 215
Sombor-Subotica 17
Speed cameras 28, 219
Stavropol 28, 29
Steak and kidney pie 219
Storm Agatha 182, 186, 191, 193, 197
Suceviţa 21, 22
Sumatra 81, 83, 85, 90, 98, 104, 113
Sumbawa-Besar 85, 93, 96, 98, 104
Switzerland 3, 10-13
Sydney 4, 8, 81, 110, 113, 119-122, 124, 218

Taft del Valle 123
Taganga 167, 172
Tandil 122, 123, 129, 130
Tanggu 59, 65-67
Tash Rabat 39, 40, 42, 43, 47, 48
Tecate 198, 202, 204, 205
Ténéré (Yamaha) 5, 27, 79, 81, 96, 101, 112, 113, 159, 176, 179, 194, 219
Terracotta Army 60, 61, 71
Thailand 3-5, 70, 73, 77, 78, 85

Tianjin 50, 59, 67
Tianshui 56, 61
Timişoara 20, 21, 23
Timor-Leste 3, 83, 101, 106, 107, 110
Ti Tree Roadhouse 112, 120
Tocopilla 149, 151, 152
Tocumen 167, 176-178
Tonalá 198
Trujillo 153
Turbo 167, 169, 170, 172, 173
Turner Valley 214
Turpan City 52, 53, 60
Tuxtla Gutierrez 198, 201

Ukraine 3, 20, 25-28, 32, 38, 54, 192
UNESCO 13, 15, 60, 88, 139
United States of America 3, 204, 207, 211
Ürümqi 52, 57
Ushuaia 123, 130, 133, 135, 137, 159

Vaccinations 6
Valley Union 123
Verona 11
Villa La Angostra 133, 137, 139
Visa applications 8, 9
Voineasa Valley 20, 23, 24

Watarrka National Park 118
West Timor 85, 101, 104
West Wyalong 116
Wuwei 66, 69

Xiahe 56, 60, 61
Xinjiang Uyghur Autonomous Region 57

Yamaha Fazer 4
Yamaha Ténéré XT660 5, 27, 79, 81, 96, 101, 112, 113, 159, 176, 179, 194, 219
Yellowstone National Park 206, 209
Yining 57

Zapala 123, 137
Zhambyl 32
Zhangyc 60, 69
Zharkent 32, 49, 50, 55, 56, 59
Zihuantanejo 198, 202, 203
Zion National Park 206, 207

More great adventure and travel bo

Packing a tent, some snacks, and a suit (!) Kevin Turner set off on a two-wheeled adventure across Europe – and had the time of his life!

Paperback • 21x14.8cm • £12.99* • 144 pages • 129 colour & b&w images • ISBN 9781845843991

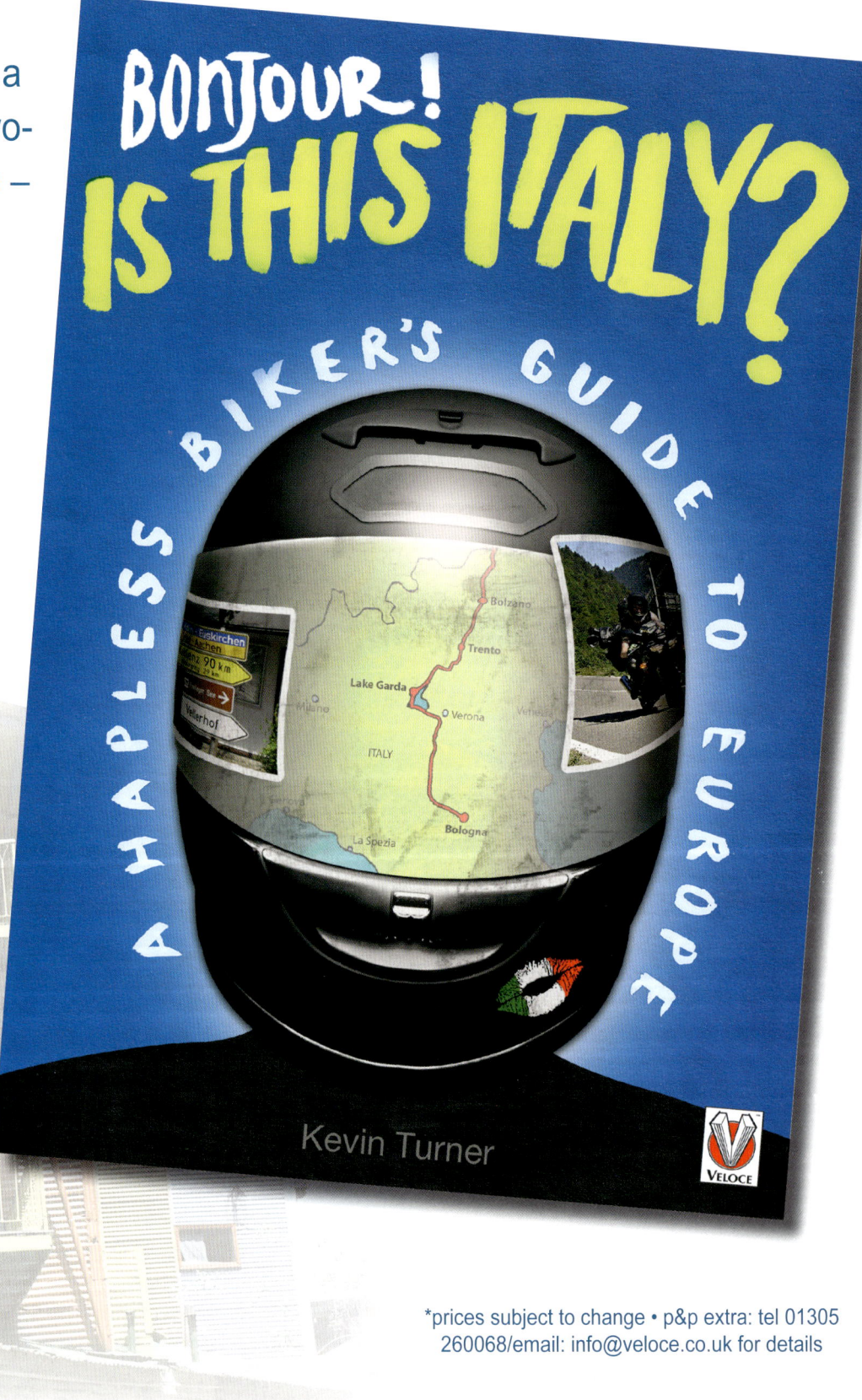

*prices subject to change • p&p extra: tel 01305 260068/email: info@veloce.co.uk for details